PATIOS, TERRACES, DECKS,
AND ROOF GARDENS

PATIOS, TERRACES, DECKS, and ROOF GARDENS

Alice Upham Smith, L.A.

WITH DRAWINGS AND DIAGRAMS BY THE AUTHOR

A Helen Van Pelt Wilson Book

HAWTHORN BOOKS, INC.
PUBLISHERS
New York

To Eastman Smith, my husband and severest
critic, this book is lovingly dedicated.

CONTENTS

For Comfortable Living Out of Doors

THE TERMS "patio" and "terrace" are used interchangeably, if inexactly, these days to refer to an outdoor living area that is usually paved. It can be any size from a private sun trap for one person to a pavement large enough for a dance; sometimes it is simply a smooth enclosed piece of lawn with chairs under a tree. Wooden decks are popular for extended living space outside, and rooftops may be designed as outdoor rooms.

As we have more leisure the patio or terrace becomes almost essential to the enjoyment of life in the garden, and an important element of landscape design. In many cases it is almost an extension of the house, adding space for the casual entertaining we all enjoy so much. The outdoor living area can suit the needs of the particular family, as a play place for children, a place for peaceful relaxing, a setting for friendly parties, or all three.

Although life on the patio may be casual, the area will be more beautiful and enjoyable if the plan for it is thought out in every detail before it is built and landscaped. Since the patio is usually seen from inside the house, it must make a pleasing picture at any time of year. There should be shade in summer, color and fragrance to add charm and gaiety, and some evergreens for year-round interest.

Down-to-earth practicality along with style is important. Plants which are easy to care for and do not litter the ground with leaves or fruit are best. Any paving that lets grass and weeds grow between the joints is unsightly and time-consuming as well.

Consider the many ways available for making life comfortable outside on the ground or on the roof: fixtures for garden lighting, sprays and electronic insect-killers, gas and electric barbecues, and outdoor fireplaces for cool evenings. Efficient storage units take care of outdoor supplies, and weatherproof carpeting makes a terrace soft under foot. The cool and soothing sound of running water can be produced by a circulating pump the size of your fist. The smallest patio can have its fountain.

To be really livable a patio needs privacy. Screen out noises and distracting views. There are various ways to achieve privacy even on a suburban lot without building a high fence all around the space, so that you may still enjoy vistas and breezes.

The addition of a well-designed terrace helps to give a house a custom-built look. It adds to the real-estate value as well as to your comfort and pleasure. The design and construction of the terrace should, of course, blend with the material and design of the house. Insofar as possible, paving should be the same as, or related to, brick, stone, or concrete used in foundations, walls, chimneys, or walks. This ties the terrace to the house and makes both a harmonious unit of the whole landscaping picture. For Contemporary and Early American houses there is a wide choice of design and material; for Georgian and Regency styles a more formal treatment is in order.

This book is intended as a practical guide to creating a functioning and beautiful patio, terrace, deck, or roof garden, whether you design and build it yourself or call in a professional. Every phase of planning, planting, maintenance, and use is considered in detail.

Alice Upham Smith

Mountain Home, Arkansas

Part One

PATIOS, TERRACES, AND DECKS

1

Fitting the Patio into the Landscape

YOUR FIRST CONSIDERATION must be where to place an outdoor living area. In many new homes sliding glass doors opening from family room or dining room make the location obvious. A terrace there next to the house will in all likelihood be also conveniently close to the kitchen, an important consideration for entertaining. It will make an always attractive picture from inside, adding interest and a sense of space to the room, and inviting one to move about.

This charming terrace of a New England house offers an irresistible invitation to enjoy living outdoors. Every comfort is offered—sun, shade, chairs for reading and resting, a table for dining—as well as the convenience of a door to the house. Setting, plantings, and furnishings are harmonious for a terrace of flagstone laid level with the lawn. *George Taloumis photo*

A California terrace with a dramatic planting is built on two levels, a swimming pool making a third. The terrace offers comfort with great elegance and opportunity to sit either in sun or in shade. Plants overhanging a pool are attractive provided they do not shed leaves. *Hort-Pix*

If there is not space enough for a patio next to a door—due to some natural feature, such as the slope of the land, a large tree, or a rocky ledge—you can make a little garden picture just outside the window. From this a path can lead to an area where there is room to spread out in comfort. The picture could be created with a birdbath under a tree, a statue or Japanese lantern, a rustic bench, a small pool, perhaps a millstone set in the path to turn the paving at an angle. Any of these would make a logical reason for moving the terrace over a bit.

A gentle slope can be either cut back from the house or filled, depending on whether the grade goes up or down. Cutting into the slope makes possible a retaining wall to sit on. A wall sixteen to eighteen inches high is just right. A higher wall could serve as the back for a bench, as background for a wall fountain, or for espaliered trees.

Building up a slope to add width to any pavement next to a house will make a more generous setting for the house. The necessary retaining walls and steps will give interest to the over-all design. Perhaps they can provide a raised bed for flowers and shrubs that will be easy to care for with no back-bending.

Terraces are not a new aspect of landscaping. This delightful area of brick in back of the eighteenth-century Raleigh Tavern in Williamsburg, Virginia, indicates that outdoor living has long been appreciated. *Colonial Williamsburg photo*

In Spain and Italy, atriums with pools and potted plants provide a garden for every room in the house and the sound of water so pleasant in a hot climate. *George Taloumis photo*

FOR A RECTANGULAR HOUSE

The average suburban lot with a rectangular house offers opportunity for various sizes and shapes of patios. Let the location of existing trees or the contour of the land influence the shape. Shape may also be determined by your preference for a certain paving material. It is easier to employ rectangular blocks in designs with straight edges. Concrete can be poured into any shape or form. If the property has no point of interest around which you can plan a patio, design one with trees and shrubs so that the patio seems to fit into the landscape.

Terraces can be enjoyed in front as well as in back of a house. Here the terrace runs the full length of a Connecticut house in the country; it extends the living quarters and gives distinction to the dwelling. The change a terrace can make is obvious from the small "before" picture. *Robert Miner photos for* Home Garden

A detail of the same terrace. The risers of the steps are old railroad ties. *Robert Miner photo for* Home Garden

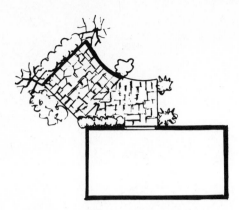

Swing the patio over to the side and cut it into a bank.

An evergreen at each corner makes it more interesting.

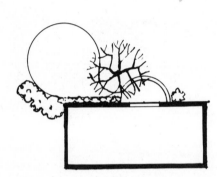

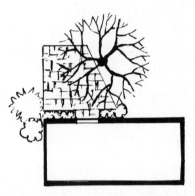

To avoid a tree, swing a large circle out to one side.

Cut the patio on a slant to avoid a tree.

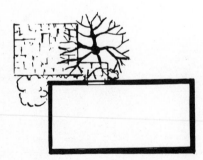

Move the patio to one side to avoid a tree beside the door.

An interesting simple plan

A patio can be placed just outside a door or can be moved to one side where there is more room.

For an L-shaped House

An L-shaped house, or one with wide-angled wings, offers an ideal place for a terrace in the corner between the two wings. Here again, there is opportunity for variety in the shape and size of the paved area. The facing wings give privacy and protection from wind. While it is good in cool climates to have a sun trap for spring and fall, it is wise to have the terrace reach beyond the corners of the house to catch the prevailing breeze in summer. In hot climates locating the terrace in the angle on the shady side of the house makes it comfortable for a greater part of the year. The house walls partly enclosing the terrace provide a decorative background for vine-covered trellises, window boxes, wall fountains, and large specimen plants. There is also the possibility of roofing over all or part of the terrace if you wish.

A patio in front of the house is a pleasant place to sit and watch for the mailman or read the evening paper. Here a euonymus vine against the wall and a lilac and Japanese yew at the side make a simple but effective planting. *Photography by Wells*

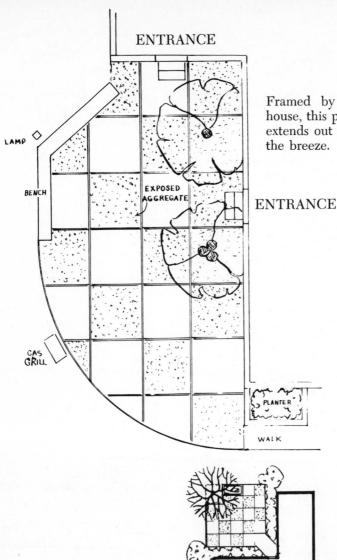

ENTRANCE

LAMP

BENCH

EXPOSED
AGGREGATE

ENTRANCE

GAS
GRILL

PLANTER

WALK

Framed by two sides of the
house, this patio has privacy yet
extends out far enough to catch
the breeze.

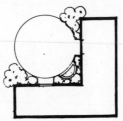

Extend patio to get the
breezes.

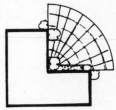

Make it fit the shape of
the property.

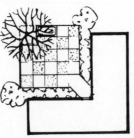

In a cold climate make
a sun trap.

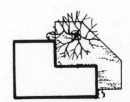

A curve is always pleas-
ing.

The wings of an L-shaped
house make an ideal set-
ting for a patio. Let the design flow out in curves and
angles.

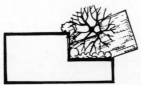

An odd angle is intrigu-
ing.

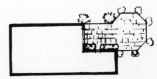

Put the main part of the
patio out in the garden.

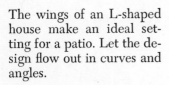

AWAY FROM THE HOUSE

There is often excellent reason for building a patio at a distance from the house. Perhaps there is a corner of the lot with a beautiful old tree that seems to call out for a terrace. Or maybe the only available level space is down at one end of your property. A view of water or mountains or some special vista offers the best possible reason for moving a living area out farther from the house. On a small narrow lot placing the terrace at the far end of the property will make a garden seem larger. A swimming pool definitely needs a patio. If only one can be built, put the paving alongside the pool, and make the area extensive enough for the various activities there. When a paved patio is at a distance from the house, let a paved pathway, reasonably wide, lead to it.

Open to the bright California sunshine but protected by two sides of the house, this informal outdoor living room with a grass "floor" is accessible from several rooms via flagstone paths. *Josef Muench photo*

Cutting back the slope made room for this patio with a retaining wall built just the right height for sitting. The overhead trellis of wrought iron matches the trim on the house. Soon vines will cover the top to give shade at midday. Designed by author. *Speidel photo*

The space between the wings of this L-shaped cottage is ideal for a patio and the low sitting wall ties it to the house (Alice Ireys, L.A.). *Molly Adams photo*

The foundation of an old mill is the setting for a sunken garden with a terrace at one end.

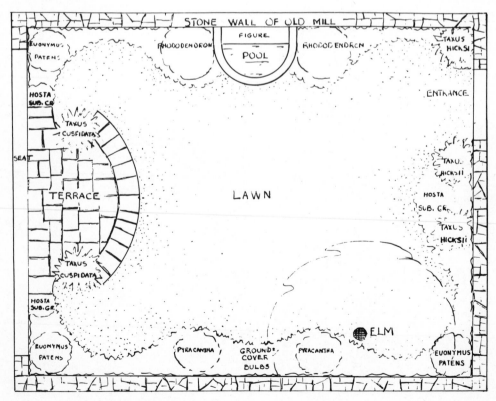

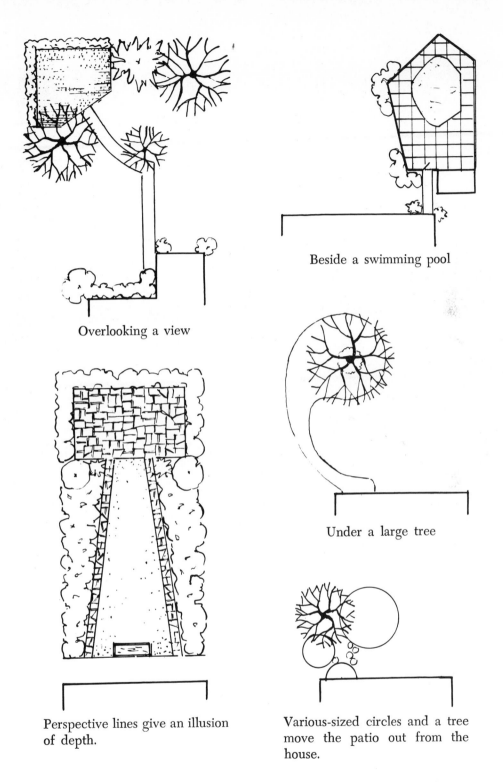

Overlooking a view

Beside a swimming pool

Under a large tree

Perspective lines give an illusion of depth.

Various-sized circles and a tree move the patio out from the house.

Patios are sometimes better placed at a distance from the house.

25

A walk from the house leads out to this patio with its splendid view of Lake Norfork in Arkansas. The paving is plain concrete so that any snake which may come up from the woods below can be readily seen. An oak shades the area for a good part of the day. *Cartie photo*

OUT IN FRONT

Sometimes the area in front of the house seems to be the only available spot for a patio, or the best place for one because of a view or good shade. Or the architecture of the house or the slope of the land may call for a terrace in front. Think of a dignified Georgian house with a broad terrace outlined by a balustrade, or a Southern home with a columned veranda spreading out onto a terrace shaded by live oaks. A contemporary house may have an entrance court. What is logical will look best.

In the country where there is enough distance from the road to give privacy, a paved living area in front can be most inviting and a

26

Built for fun, this gay little summer house adjoins a half-circle patio and offers shade or shelter from a sudden shower. *George Taloumis photo*

gracious setting for the house. In the country the space at the back may be needed for a vegetable garden, garage, or barns. Then there is no other pleasant place for a terrace but at the front.

Many modern houses are built with a picture window facing the street, and often the "picture" is simply a view of the street—monotonous or worse. Furthermore, the big window gives no privacy unless curtains are pulled across the glass. If a terrace is built just outside, taking up part of the lawn area in front, and set off by a low hedge, fence, or wall, the window is justified and has an outlook that can be interesting throughout the year. Some of the foundation plants can then be pulled forward and, from within, the room will appear to expand outward. Viewed from the street, the horizontal lines of hedge, fence, or low wall give a restful look to the house.

Several small flowering trees can be placed to emphasize the sense of separation from the street and contribute some shade to the terrace. Even on a corner lot, peace, quiet, and beauty can be achieved for outdoor living by planting borders of evergreen and deciduous shrubs. These must be set well back from the street to avoid obstructing the view of drivers.

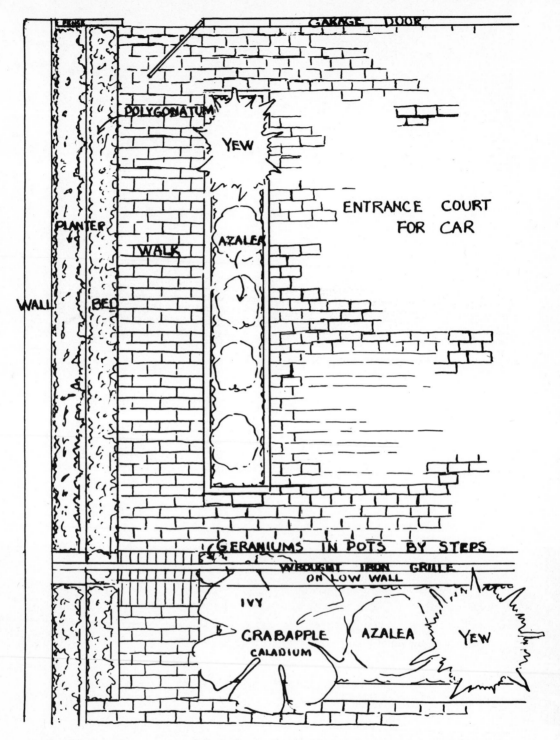

In this entrance courtyard, a bed of yew and azaleas separates the walk from the car area. More planting shields the upper patio from the garage, as shown on page 38, bottom left.

At some little distance from the house is this bird-watcher's deck-and-flagstone terrace. Feeders are suspended from a Japanese plum-tree. A reflecting pool takes the overflow from an artesian well and offers "open" water to birds in winter. *Molly Adams photo*

A swimming pool tucked into the side of a hill leaves room for a narrow brick terrace for sun-bathing and lounging. *Photography by Wells*

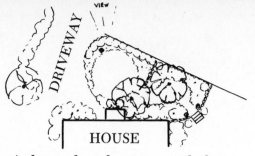

A dooryard garden-patio overlooking a view

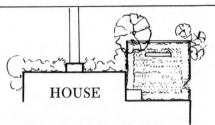

A sunny, convenient location in front

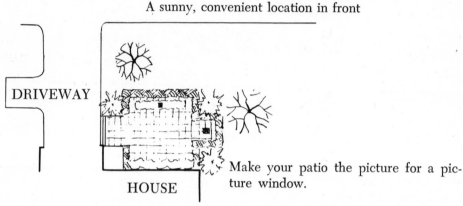

Make your patio the picture for a picture window.

Locate the patio in front of the house if that is the logical place for it.

The dooryard garden, a heritage of our New England ancestors, is growing in popularity, and the dooryard is certainly a delightful place for a terrace, especially for a Colonial cottage. Then all the beauty and livability of the garden can be concentrated at the front of the house. A brick terrace and white picket fence, set off by beds of bright flowers and some boxwood or yew, make a little place that is pleasant to behold from inside or out. Wrought iron and blue-stone with clipped evergreens make a more imposing dooryard garden for a dignified house.

The entrance court that ties in with garage or carport offers another possibility. A high wall or fence with an ornamental gate can shut off the patio on the street side and thus give privacy to most of the lower windows of the house. An entrance court requires a formal planting that looks well all year, a paving that is easy to clear of ice and snow, and a well-thought-out plan that considers primarily the functional purposes.

30

Atriums and Private Patios

Some contemporary homes are now built around an enclosed court or atrium. The paving and planting of such a place should compliment the interior decoration of the house as well as the style of the architecture. Brick, tile, or carpeting can run from one or more rooms out to the atrium with no break. Of course, good drainage is essential in the court. In such a sheltered spot exotic plants can be grown. A planter set half inside the house and half outside in the atrium can closely associate garden and house. But completely enclosing the patio will make it hot unless openings are planned for a good circulation of air straight through the house.

Where a special patio is built for a master bedroom or other room it is usually small and screened by a tall fence to assure privacy. It is usually entered only from that one room. Sometimes it is built to screen out a poor view or a nearby house. In any case, such a small patio can be one of the most delightful of all if it is well planned.

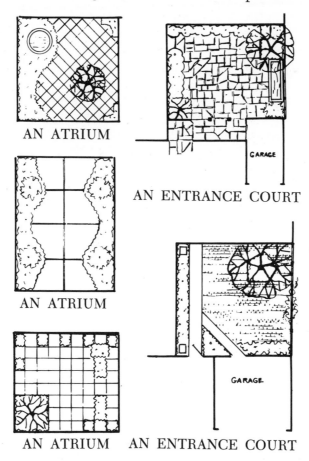

AN ATRIUM

AN ENTRANCE COURT

AN ATRIUM

AN ATRIUM   AN ENTRANCE COURT

On the left are three plans for atriums; on the right, two designs for entrance courts.

31

2

Ways to Extend an Existing Patio

WHEN A NEW HOUSE IS BUILT, the contractor often puts in a small rectangle of concrete for a patio outside the back door or the sliding doors to the family room. This is a move in the right direction; at least a flat dry space invites stepping outdoors and provides a link between house and garden. However, the rectangular space is rarely large enough for family and friends to gather on for a cookout, or for children to play there in wet weather. It is also completely lacking in interest, beauty, shade, or privacy. The uncompromising shape and solidity of a paved rectangle seem to make any kind of addition a problem, but there are various easy ways to extend such an existing patio.

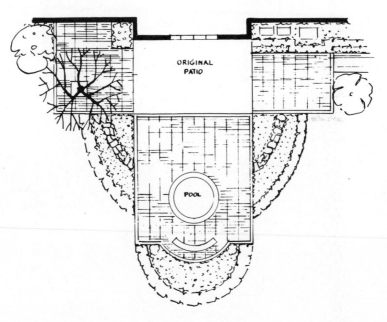

Here a small concrete terrace is the nucleus for extensions—left, right, and forward—that can be made through the years.

Above, a patio, with a small pool mounted by a figure and trees planted in areas left open for them, is made colorful with pots of petunias: 'Rose Star,' 'Coral Cascade,' 'White Cascade,' 'Paleface,' 'Sugar Daddy,' 'Red Magic,' and 'Fandango.' *Below,* the same patio, featuring rocks and petunias in a secluded area. *Pan-American Seed Co. photos*

Above, extensive roof garden at Kaiser Center in Berkeley (Osmundson and Staley, L.A.) and (*below*) a charming home patio.

Above, an interesting contrast in flooring and (*below*) a handsome entrance court with accents of tall flowering shrubs, all in California (Theodore Osmundson, L.A.). *Osmundson photos*

Above, a patio built for the enjoyment of a vast California panorama (Thomas D. Church, L.A.) and (*below*) a small comfortable atrium in Honolulu.

Generally speaking, an outdoor living area should be about the size of the main living room. Then it will be in scale with the house. It can be larger so long as it is not designed as one solid sheet of paving, but rather divided into areas by low plants or grass.

ENLARGING A CONCRETE SLAB

The obvious way to enlarge an existing concrete patio is to add more concrete paving. Draw some designs on paper, then try them out on the ground. Lay a garden hose to help you visualize curves. If the ground is level, any pattern that has visual impact will be pleasing. In some cases the slope of the ground will influence the pattern.

A patio can be extended in various ways.

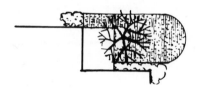

A change of material makes the addition more interesting.

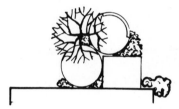

Add two circles and a tree to shade them.

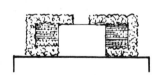

Two brick side areas with hedges add needed space.

Circles combined with straight lines. Add a pool and a tree.

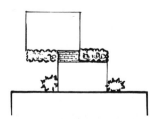

A brick wall and hedges on both sides provide a transition.

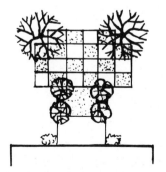

Side planting links the old patio to the addition.

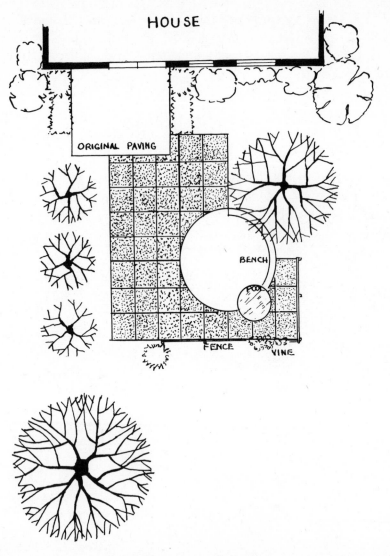

The circle of concrete in the addition of exposed aggregate squares repeats both the material and the approximate size of the original patio. A small pool is a focal point. A six-foot-high fence on two sides and flowering trees on the third insure privacy. Designed by the author. *Permission of* Woman's Day

Combine areas of plain and patterned concrete. This is fun especially in contemporary designs where a plan can be worked out in two or three textures. Sometimes merely grooving one part of the concrete into squares will give enough change of texture. Concrete set in four-foot or larger squares and outlined by two-by-four redwood strips is attractive and easy, since a square or two can be done at a time by anyone who likes to work in concrete.

34

Aggregate with Stones for Texture

In mild climates exposed aggregate with the stones showing on top of the concrete gives warmth and color and avoids the glare from plain concrete in strong sunshine. Aggregate is easiest to lay in small sections, and redwood strips again make excellent dividers. On such a terrace, also use redwood for a bench or a planter so that the effect will be harmonious.

Expanding a terrace can be an easy do-it-yourself project, especially with bricks or patio blocks laid in sand. The warm color of brick and variations of paving pattern suggest many pleasing designs. Brick combines well with concrete, and so do paving blocks, which come in soft tans and pinks as well as the usual gray. With brick, introduce more plain concrete into the design by putting a rim of it around a pool or adding a concrete bench or planter. This will help relate the original slab of paving to the larger design.

Set any new paving about four feet out from the house to leave space for the softening and cooling effect of shrubbery planted close to the house. If the new area is extensive, leave an open space in the paving for a tree. A tree will not only provide shade but also cast shadowy patterns.

The brick-and-flagstone paving in this entrance court is separated by a wide low step. The yews, ilex, and ivy are tolerant of city conditions, as is the Japanese maple, which is silouetted against the wall. *George Taloumis photo*

Emphasizing a Transition

Make a virtue of necessity and emphasize the transition from the original slab to the new area. An old millstone might make a pivot for a design to turn in any direction. A small pool could be helpful in the same way and also enjoyable from both the old and the new section. Leave room around it for a ruffle of green or some flowers. Rocks set in a mosaic pattern or flat rocks and gravel could serve as a nice transition. For an entrance to an informal terrace, use gravel outlined with railroad ties, and for stepping stones, rounds cut from a tree.

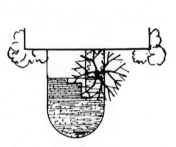

A pool and a bench make a transition.

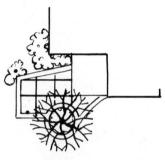

A band of concrete ties the old and the new sections.

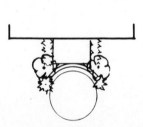

Broad steps lead down to an addition.

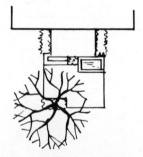

Steps and a pool make a gradual change of grade.

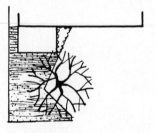

A larger brick area is added at an odd angle.

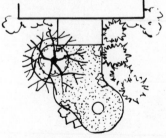

An informal area harmonizes patio and a natural garden.

An easy but definite transition can be worked out between the original patio and the addition.

DESIGN ON TWO LEVELS

Even with sloping ground, patios can be extended by designing them on two levels. A two-foot change is not bad. Steps leading from one level to another can combine two paving materials, such as brick with concrete, railroad ties with brick, or flagstone steps with concrete risers. Making the steps generous in length and gradual in rise seems to bring the two levels closer together.

A retaining wall could make extra seating for a lower terrace, and also provide a raised bed for trailing plants or a fountain and pool. Planters on several levels or large pots of flowers on the steps would add interest and be an invitation to go up or down. If the slope is very steep, continue building out the terrace with a deck to gain as much level room as possible. The greater the paved area, the more livable is the garden in all kinds of weather, and the easier it is to care for.

Changing the pattern of paving and dividing the areas make this beautiful garden of Alice Ireys, a landscape architect, more interesting, and it seems larger, too. *Molly Adams photo*

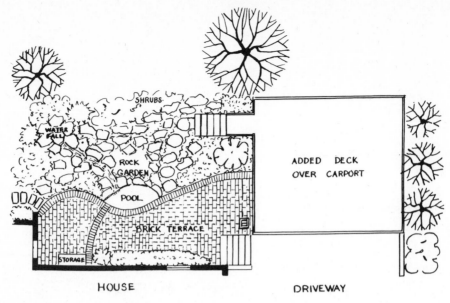

A deck adds to the living space, as shown in this design for the garden on page 61.

On a city property, a wrought-iron grille separates a parking area from an upper terrace. Double planters filled with ivy, geraniums, ferns, and Solomon's-seal soften the high brick wall; a flowering crabapple and a bed of Japanese yews, azaleas, and caladiums decorate the terrace next to the house. *George Taloumis photo*

A small city patio in spring is charming with pale yellow tulips and white dogwood and andromeda, and all these do well in the shade. The bamboo screen at the rear makes an interesting textural contrast to the over-all brick, and pots and beds set into the paving hold a considerable number of plants (Alice Ireys, L.A.). *George Taloumis photo*

For a garden view outside a bedroom, what could be more charming than this small, very private Japanese-style patio? The plants are Baltic ivy and *Euonymus vegetus*, the materials two kinds of gravel with brick. A louvered fence lets in air. *Photography by Wells*

3

Making the Most of Limited Space

THE OPPOSITE PROBLEM to extending a patio is that of making the most of limited space in a city garden or small private area, perhaps off a bedroom. To make the available space count, extend the patio to the limit of the property and then enclose it with a fence or wall. Surprising as it may seem, enclosing an area makes it seem larger. However, a fence while providing privacy should also admit circulation of air. Fences with baffles or spaces between boards, brick, or concrete block laid with openings between, are all effective. Look for old pieces of ornamental iron grille to set in an opening. A wire or chain-link fence with vines will also let air through.

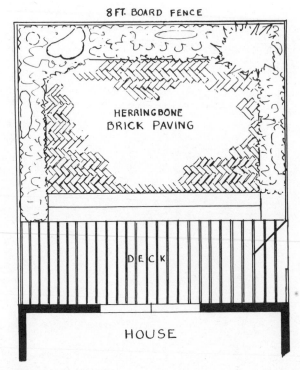

This patio, including the deck, is only twenty feet square. Wide steps and the herringbone pattern of brick make it seem larger. The fence is eight feet high. The photograph appears on page 55.

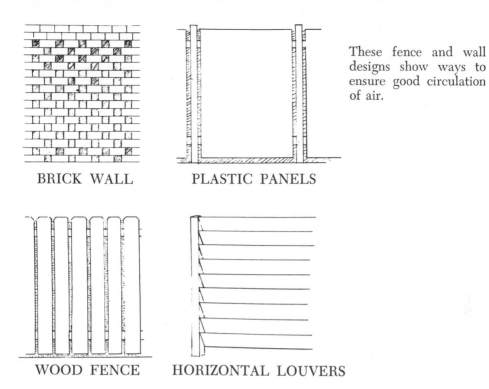

BRICK WALL **PLASTIC PANELS**

These fence and wall designs show ways to ensure good circulation of air.

WOOD FENCE **HORIZONTAL LOUVERS**

Even a tiny patio like this one under an old apple tree with a floor of red brick squares set in small white stones can give much pleasure. Outside the kitchen door, it is a most pleasant place for summer meals.

In a small area, use as much green as possible for its softening effect. Vines are a good choice, since they take up little room in proportion to the foliage they produce. If there is no space for a tree, or none nearby to give shade, a vine on an overhead trellis will provide some shade.

Ground-covers can carpet all unpaved areas with luxuriant green. The texture of Baltic ivy, ajuga, periwinkle, or pachysandra shows up well next to paving. Since paving reduces the number of plants needed, the money saved can be spent on a few fine specimens of just a few varieties, including the ground-cover. Limiting the kinds of material will give an uncluttered effect. Espaliered shrubs or small trees are interesting all year.

To relieve the green, you can add color and fragrance with potted plants or hanging baskets filled with tuberous begonias or trailing fuchsias. Urns of tulips or hyacinths in spring followed by such summer annuals as petunias, and then with chrysanthemums in fall will give continuous color. Burying pots in the ground keeps earth in them from drying out quickly and less frequent watering is needed. Lilies grow well in pots and make a spectacular show in a small place.

This tiny circular dining patio is especially enjoyable when the wisteria is in fragrant bloom. *Mattie Edwards Hewitt photo*

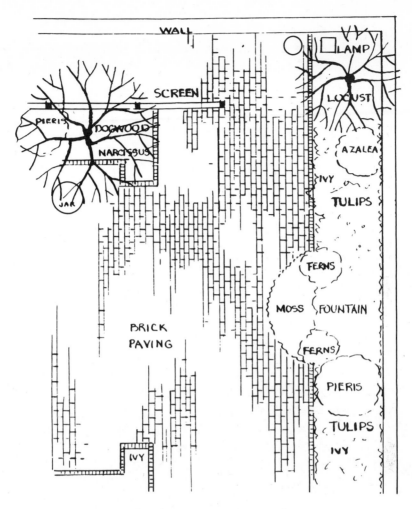

A plan for a patio on a city lot

Bricks laid in curving patterns make an attractive design for the floor of this two-level patio with steps for easy transition (Friede Stege, L.A.). *Molly Adams photo*

WATER—A COOLING DEVICE

The sound of splashing water does wonders for a small enclosed patio. To save space let the house or the garden wall serve as background for a wall fountain with a pool at the base. Features that do double duty conserve space. For children, make a small sand box that can be covered over to make a low table, or put the sand in a low pit that later can become a pool, a fire pit, or a flower bed. A raised bed for plants could have a wide border of wood or brick to provide more seating space when there are guests.

It is most important in planning a small patio to understand that the more limited the space, the simpler the plan must be. Each element should be a jewel. The small courtyard can be a restful, well-ordered oasis in a busy world.

A pool and jet fountain make an interesting low water feature that does not cut off the view beyond. *Photography by Wells*

4

Layout and Construction

FUNDAMENTAL IN BUILDING A PATIO are accuracy in laying the outline and good construction work.

First, plan your patio carefully on paper, figuring out all measurements both of design and grades. Use graph paper allowing one square on the paper to so many feet on the ground. All measurements should

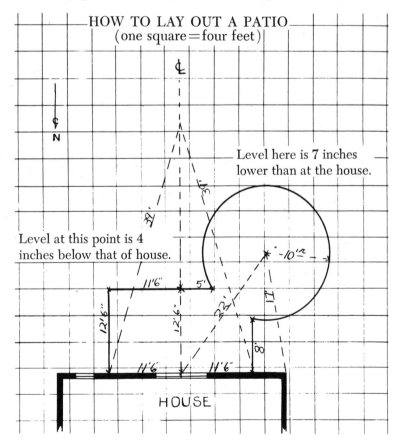

Design a patio on graph paper. Find a center at a given point. Construct center line by making a triangle with equal sides. Find any center of radius by making a triangle. The same measurements can be put on the ground afterward.

start from a known point, such as the corner of the house, or a window that may be the central viewing point of the design.

Draw any curves on the plan with a compass, and mark the center of the radius on the plan. No matter how complex the curves are, you can figure them out with a compass and then transfer them exactly to the ground. This makes a much better design for construction work

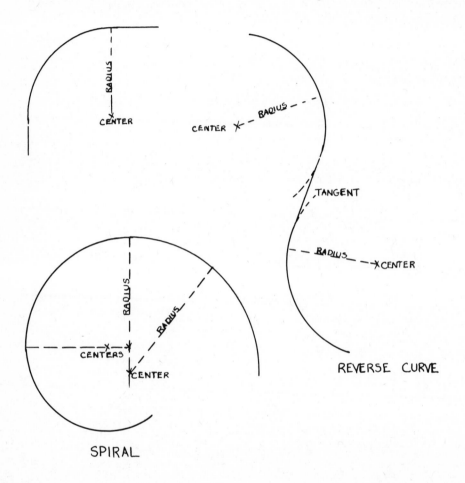

REVERSE CURVE

SPIRAL

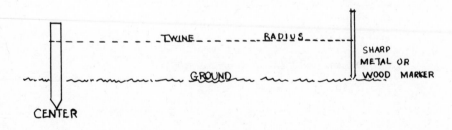

How to lay out curves

than simply laying curves on the ground with a garden hose, useful as this may be at the idea stage. Find the center of the circle on the ground by measuring from two known points, as shown on the plan. The center of the circle will be where the lines intersect.

Drive a sharp stake at the center. Measure a piece of mason's twine to correspond with the radius; tie one end to the stake. Keeping the line taut, mark the circumference with a sharp stick as you walk around it. This way you can outline the curve.

Make all straight lines parallel or perpendicular to the house (unless the design has an odd angle that has been specifically measured off). Construct a center line for the design. To do this, measure equal distances to each side from the point where the line will start. Drive a stake at the center point and at each side point. Tie lines to the side stakes. Measure the same number of feet on each line.

Pull the lines tight, and make a mark on the ground about where the center line will come. The point at which the marks intersect will be the *exact* center of the center line. Drive a stake at that point and run a line between the center stakes on the lawn. You will then have an accurate center line from which to make all measurements.

Mark the outline of the patio on the ground, using stakes and twine. Use boards to indicate the boundaries. To curve a board, saw a two-by-four or two-by-six halfway through every few inches so that it will bend easily. The greener the wood, the more pliable it will be.

Establishing the Grade

Now that you have made the outline, it is time to establish the grade. If the ground where the patio is to be built has been filled, let it settle for at least six months before paving, otherwise the paving will settle and crack. Paving should slope one-quarter inch for each foot out from the house, or from end to end if it is free-standing. That would make a five-inch drop for twenty feet. Surprisingly, the slope will not be noticeable.

To get an accurate level, drive two stakes, one at the house, and one at the far end of the patio area. Draw a length of mason's twine very taut between the two stakes. Fasten a line level (from the hardware store) in the center of the twine. Get the line absolutely level. Now drop the far end the required number of inches; for example, five inches for twenty feet.

The bottom grade should be about six inches below the top

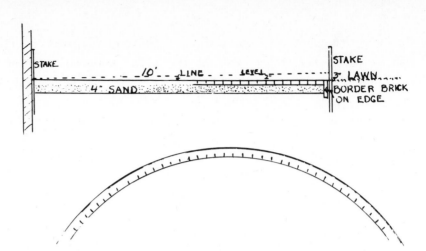

To grade a patio, pull a line level between stakes. Drop it at the far end—one-quarter inch per foot. Excavate six inches for sand and brick. Make the far edge of the patio level with the lawn. To curve a form, make a series of cuts halfway through a wet or green two-by-four.

grade. If the ground is wet or soft, make the bottom grade still lower to allow for a fill of four inches of gravel and two inches of sand below the grade of the paving material. Ordinarily, on firm ground, four inches of sand makes a sound base for brick paving.

Large decorative urns of geraniums make handsome accents on walls, and pots of flowers on the steps set the stage for a warm welcome. *George Taloumis photo*

If there is to be no wall at the edge of the patio, paving should end at lawn-level. Then grass at the edge can easily be trimmed by running the lawn-mower along it.

Paving materials offer many possibilities for designs in different colors and textures; there is certainly no need to have a monotonous piece of paving. Brick, tile, rectangular concrete patio blocks, concrete either plain or textured, and slate flagstones can be mixed and matched to make various patterns. In some parts of the country treated wood blocks or rounds are available for paving.

PAVING WITH BRICK OR PATIO BLOCKS

Brick is easy for an amateur to lay, and is the least expensive of all paving materials. Brick comes in shades of pink, red, russet, and sometimes buff, and there are also used bricks with mellow mottled effects. Four and one-half bricks will cover one square foot of paving.

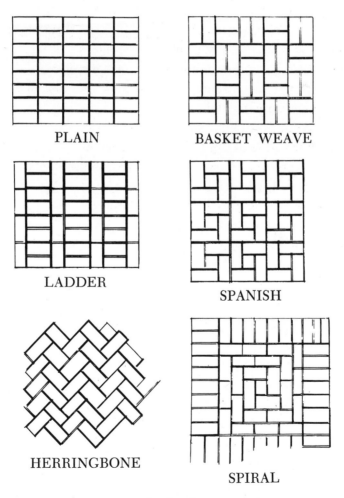

PLAIN   BASKET WEAVE

LADDER   SPANISH

HERRINGBONE   SPIRAL

49

Six patterns for brick paving

Interspersing squares of concrete in a large expanse of brick paving gives it more character. Designed by Robert E. Goetz, L.A. *Goetz photo*

The quickest way to lay bricks is in a plain pattern of parallel lines. But many other paving patterns are fun to lay once the design is started, and all patterns take the same number of bricks. Even curves work out well with brick, and repetition enhances the curved lines. The texture and color of brick look well with wood.

Concrete patio blocks are two inches deep and eight-by-sixteen inches across. They come in gray, tan, and pink. Because of their size the job of laying them is relatively fast.

To lay brick or patio blocks, first prepare a level area to the right depth. Put in four inches of sand. Order twice as much sand as the number of cubic yards you estimate you will need, because sand packs down. Tamp the sand well, wet it, and let it settle overnight.

Now spread another half-inch of sand, but only over the area on which you will be immediately laying bricks. Lay the bricks one by one, tamping each one down tight with a board and hammer so that they will be well packed. Don't strike bricks directly with a hammer for they will chip. When you have laid several rows, put a board on top, and tamp all the bricks down together.

Be sure joints are tight. Check the level frequently. Lay the final row of bricks on end, make a mortared border, or set one-by-six redwood boards on edge.

When you have finished the paving, spread several shovelfuls of sand over the bricks, sweep it into the joints, and water with a fine spray. Repeat if necessary to fill all the cracks. You may have to do this again the next year.

50

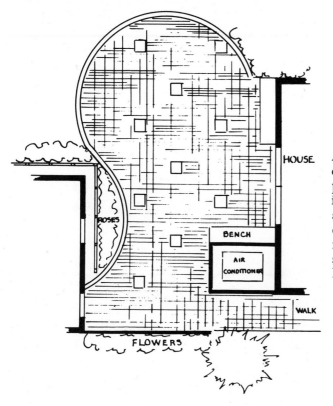

FENCE

HOUSE

ROSES

BENCH

AIR CONDITIONER

WALK

FLOWERS

A fence conceals the air conditioner and also gives privacy. Large squares set in the brick paving make an interesting pattern. A curve by the garage allows room for a rose trellis. Designed by Robert E. Goetz, L.A.

Concrete Paving

Concrete makes the most permanent paving, and requires the least maintenance. In cold climates it should always be strengthened with wire fencing or reinforcing rods. Concrete requires good drainage underneath; spread a three- to four-inch layer of crushed rock or cinders as a foundation. Two-by-fours make excellent forms to assure straight edges.

If you are doing the paving yourself, it will be easier to lay the patio in squares or rectangles outlined by redwood or treated two-by-fours. Then you can do one small section at a time. For a larger area of unbroken concrete, insert expansion joints every six to eight feet. Be sure the final height of the paving comes level with the lawn.

There are various ways of finishing concrete. You can mark squares or designs on it with grooves. It can be made of one solid color,

51

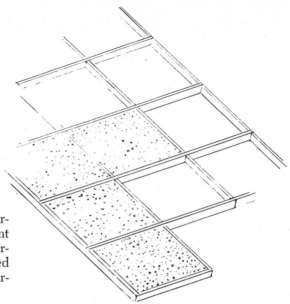

A grid of two-by-fours in four-foot squares makes an excellent form for pouring concrete flooring. The concrete can be poured in sections at convenient intervals.

as green, or be multicolored for a modern design. In bright sun, smooth concrete is unpleasantly glaring, so it is a good idea to have texture. In mild climates, you can get texture with exposed aggregate, that is, letting the gravel-mix show on the surface. Add pebbles of the color and size you wish directly to the mix, or press them into the top layer as soon as the concrete is poured. When the concrete is almost set, sweep it so that the pebbles show, then clean it with a fine spray of water.

Exposed aggregate combined with squares of plain concrete makes an interesting contrast of textures and reduces the glare that comes from plain concrete. *Cartie photo*

If there is a brick plant near you, you can try this kind of decoration. Get some "green" bricks, draw on them, and then have them fired. *Photography by Wells*

FLAGSTONE OR GRAVEL FLOORING

Flagstone comes in soft shades with a grayish cast. Thickness varies, and sections are either cut square or irregular. You can lay flagstone in concrete three to four inches deep or in four inches of sand. Follow the procedure for brick. Irregular flagstone set in sand with grass or flowers in the spaces between makes a nice informal terrace.

A gravel patio is quick to make and inexpensive. It is also easily adaptable to any shape or size. After excavating about four inches, lay polyethelene plastic on the surface. Make a firm border of brick, cement blocks, redwood strips, or metal. Then fill with small crushed stone, ending with a top inch of pea gravel. To give life to the monotonous color, mix in a small amount of lighter and darker gravel.

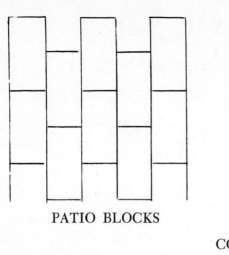

PATIO BLOCKS

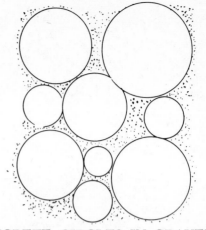

CONCRETE CIRCLES IN GRAVEL

RANDOM STONE

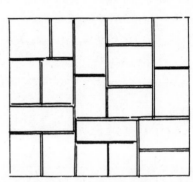

RANDOM RECTANGULAR

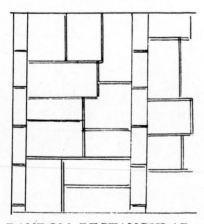

RANDOM RECTANGULAR
AND BRICK

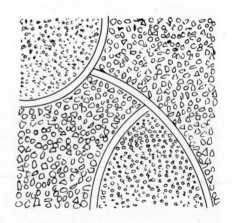

PEBBLE MOSAIC

Six patterns for paving

5

Decks, Steps, Roofs, and Walls

WOODEN DECKS blend harmoniously into the landscape. They have a warm pleasing texture, but the surface is relatively cool, due to the high insulating properties of wood. They are also resilient to walk on.

Decks are especially concordant with informal modern architecture and structural materials. They can also be quite elegant and formal, if intelligently designed. No outdoor flooring is more flexible, easily fitting any shape or series of levels, and associating well with steps and fences in the over-all plan. As to color, wood can be left to weather to a silvery gray,

Partial shade for the deck area of this small outdoor living room, for which there was no tree, is provided by a grapevine trained over a plastic awning. The brick area below is in full sun for part of the day, and an espaliered witchhazel covers the high, uncompromising board fence. *Johnston photo*

or it can be stained in various colors. Where ground slopes away from a house, a deck is an excellent solution to the problem, since it can be built out at floor-level and so avoids expensive fill.

For long-lasting decks, select redwood, pressure-treated pine, or cedar. Use two-by-threes, two-by-fours, or two-by-sixes for the floor. Lay the boards a quarter-inch apart using shims (or spacers) to keep the openings accurate. Set the supporting beams about four feet apart; use two-by-sixes or two-by-eights, depending on the length of the deck. Since rain will drain off through the spaces between boards, a deck can be made level. Wherever wood is to come into contact with the ground, treat it with preservatives. Use galvanized, aluminum, or stainless-steel nails to avoid rust marks.

On this stony California hillside, a deck is the ideal means to an outdoor living area. A broad bench holds cushions and a decorative tubbed pine. A clump of nandina ties the lower deck with the upper. *Hort-Pix*

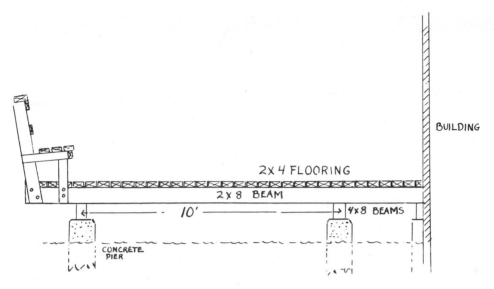

This is one kind of deck construction; treated wood posts could be used instead of piers. Here a bench is incorporated in the railing.

A very large deck extends the living area out over a slope, making a restful outdoor room with a fine view of the distant hills (Royston, Hanamoto, and Mayes, L.A.).

Brick steps lead down over an expanse of brick terrace to a parquet redwood deck of imaginative design. The structure extends out over the water to make a sitting area with a wide view of the ocean at Palm Beach, Florida. Designed by Edward D. Stone, Jr. *California Redwood Association photo*

Laced to circular metal tubing, this smart canopy hangs from a tree and emphasizes the elevated situation of the deck. *Canvas Awning Institute*

Here low junipers at the corner relate the deck to the lawn and tall viburnums to the house. Gravel is thickly spread underneath to deter weeds in a place that would be difficult to reach (Clara Coffey, L.A.). *Molly Adams photo*

In the center of a large redwood deck a fire pit with a bench around it makes a good place to sit and roast hot dogs. Designed by author.

The level area on top of a carport is a fine place to build a deck. Here entrance is through the rock garden at the left. Trees in back will soon grow enough to hide the house next door. Designed by author.

GARDEN STEPS

Steps add to the charm of a garden. Plan them so that they not only take you from one level to another but also become a feature in the design. Avoid having only one step: people are apt to stumble over it. Put in two shallow steps instead. Since there is more room outside than in, garden steps can have deeper treads and lower risers than steps inside a house. Five- to seven-inch risers and twelve- to sixteen-inch-wide treads are good. The over-all measurement of tread and riser should equal about

61

twenty-five inches for each step. The lower the riser, the deeper the tread can be; the gentler the slope, the wider the steps.

There are as many building materials for steps as there are for patios, and the steps should harmonize with the paving of a patio. Bricks and cement blocks need to be set in mortar on good foundations. Steps can be made of railroad ties or redwood strips with brick or gravel in back. Hold ties in place with stakes driven well down at each end.

Set large flat fieldstones directly on the ground. Begin building at the bottom of the flight of steps, and work up, resting each stone on the rear edge of the stone below so that it is well supported.

To look finished, steps generally need walls or wings on either side. For steep steps or long flights a railing is desirable. An electric light will make steps much safer at night.

An easy flight of garden steps

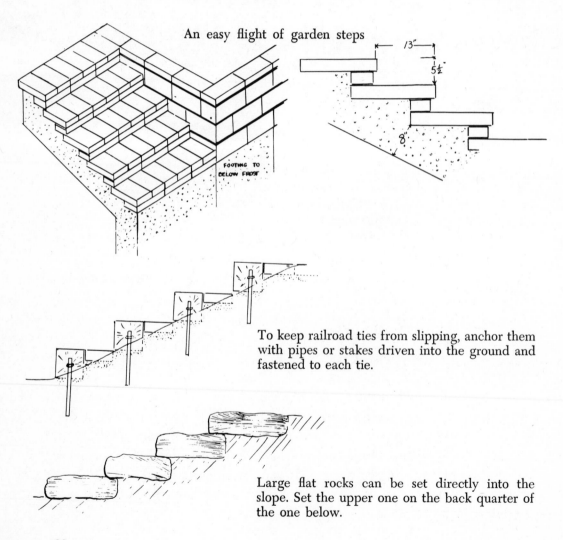

To keep railroad ties from slipping, anchor them with pipes or stakes driven into the ground and fastened to each tie.

Large flat rocks can be set directly into the slope. Set the upper one on the back quarter of the one below.

62

Shade for the Patio

A large tree in the right place provides the best shade for a patio. If there are no good-sized trees nearby and the patio gets midday and afternoon sun, a partial cover will make the area more comfortable.

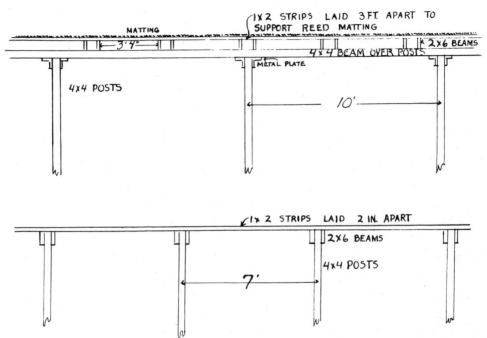

Two ways to construct a trellis. At the top is shown a strong but lightweight construction for supporting matting. The lower trellis is made of wood strips or battens to give shade.

To construct such a cover, you usually need a building permit. Check on local restrictions and then plan to make the trellis or partial roof strong. For supports, use four-by-four posts set eight to ten feet apart, or two-inch steel pipe. Work out the design primarily with the type of roofing material in mind. The roof should have openings for ventilation to prevent heat being trapped underneath.

Covering Materials for the Patio

One of the most popular coverings is woven reed or bamboo; it has nice texture, is inexpensive, and easy to install. It gives soft irregular shade, pleasant to live with. Such woven matting should be nailed to a rigid frame.

Wood laths or battens are also excellent for a cover, and louvers, either fixed or adjustable, can be slanted to block out strong sun. Louvers running east and west will cut off midday sun. North and south louvers will keep out either morning or afternoon sun.

Canvas strips make a lightweight cover. You can remove them in winter to let more light into the house through any windows opening onto the patio. The simplest way to get some shade is to buy a large canvas garden umbrella.

In wet climates, translucent or opaque Fiberglas or plastic roofings are best. These are available in flat and corrugated sheets that are lightweight and easy to install. They let in soft light and cut glare. In a cool climate, use clear or frosted panels, in a warm climate blue, green, or yellow panels are better. Be sure to leave space for ventilation at the eaves.

An egg-crate roof lets in plenty of air but also gives a sense of shelter. Direct sunlight comes through in the middle of the day, but not in the morning or afternoon. Vines are particularly nice on an egg-crate roof. They help to keep out midday sun. Vines on any overhead trellis cut down the heat since they do not re-radiate it, and the leaves and branches make shadow patterns on the paving below. Most vines are deciduous, letting in winter sun.

Woven reed or bamboo makes inexpensive, easy-to-install coverings that give soft, pleasant shade. *Photography by Wells*

64

This deck is partly shaded by an awning, whose framework is built into a long stationary bench made comfortable with cushions. These and other furnishings can be stored in the box under the bench. *Canvas Awning Institute*

An airy, tentlike structure of striped cotton canvas on a redwood frame makes a shady area for a gravel patio decorated with sunny beds of dahlias and a great lacy fern. *Canvas Awning Institute*

A canvas awning of contemporary design shades a deck that would otherwise be too open and sunny for comfort. *Canvas Awning Institute*

A flagstone terrace sheltered by a roof of translucent plastic — the panels set between beams and redwood strips—is pleasantly withdrawn from the noisy goings-on at a pool but in full view of children bathing there. *Molly Adams photo*

66

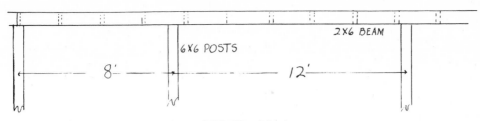

6X6 POSTS

2X6 BEAM

8'   12'

FRONT VIEW

2X6s

2 FT.
SQUARE

PLAN

An egg-crate trellis is strong, providing light shade and a strong support for vines.

A trellis of sturdy beams covered by grape and wisteria vines shades but does not cut off air from this elegant outdoor dining room with house walls on three sides. *George Taloumis photo*

Good Vines for Covering a Trellis

Anemone clematis	*Clematis montana*
Boston-ivy	*Parthenocissus tricuspidata*
Bougainvillea *	*Bougainvillea spectabilis*
Climbing roses	*Rosea* species and varieties
Grape	*Vitis* species
Honeysuckle	*Lonicera sempervirens*
Passion-vine *	*Passiflora* species
Silver-lace-vine	*Polygonum auberti*
Sweet autumn clematis	*Clematis paniculata*
Trumpet-vine	*Campsis radicans*
Virginia-creeper	*Parthenocissus quinquefolia*
Wisteria	*Wisteria* species and varieties

* Not hardy except in the South.

Low Retaining and Sitting Walls

Some kind of retaining wall is necessary to hold earth back when ground slopes down toward a patio. Even when not necessary, a wall always gives a handsome finishing touch to a patio, and adds the sense of another level. You can sit on it, set pots of flowers on it, or use it as background for a border of flowers. A wall can relate elements of a patio design by becoming part of a barbecue pit or the back of a fountain.

Laying the foundation is the most important operation in building a wall, even a low one. Set it below the frost line for your locality and make a broad footing at the base. That is what keeps a retaining wall from

A striped canvas awning supported by only one pole makes an efficient shade for an open patio by a pool. *Canvas Awning Institute*

leaning out from the pressure of earth behind it and what keeps a free-standing wall upright. To make a three-foot dry-stone retaining wall—one without mortar—set the heaviest stones at the bottom. Make the wall widest at the base, sloping the front and back in as you build it up so that the wall is nine to twelve inches narrower at the top than at the bottom.

Reinforced-concrete walls should be a minimum of ten inches thick. Curved brick walls can be four to eight inches thick, since curving makes them stronger. Provide weep holes eight inches above the grade on the lower side of any retaining wall. A wall for sitting is comfortable if it is sixteen to eighteen inches high and twelve to sixteen inches wide.

Match or blend the material of a wall with the paving of the patio and the style of the house. Concrete blocks are easy to use for a low wall. A concrete wall must have a good form into which to pour cement, but concrete is adaptable to any shape. Cement bricks come in gray, tan, and pink. They are longer and thinner than standard bricks. Railroad ties make an attractive rustic wall. Iron or cement grilles or tiles are ornamental in free-standing walls.

Interesting old metal pieces furnish the intimate terrace of a board-and-batten house in Kansas City, Missouri. Long cement bricks make the wall, which is just the right height for extra seating, and on the outside is a border of roses. An angel-wing begonia in a pot and ivy growing in the corner are pleasing accents. *Roche photo*

When the sun is too bright, a gentle pull slides this awning on overhead wires above the patio. *Canvas Awning Institute*

An openwork brick wall with a well-designed gate casts shadow patterns on a brick terrace that features a fountain figure. Designed by author. *Hansbrough photo*

A reinforced-concrete retaining wall with steps on one side is suitable for this simple concrete patio. Designed by author. *Hansbrough photo*

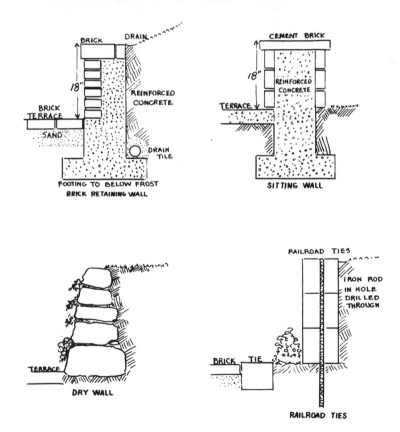

Sitting and retaining walls

71

Screening an Air Conditioner

The necessary air-conditioning unit is likely to be on or near a patio, and it needs to be screened. Some plants, among them privet, euonymus, and yucca can tolerate the stream of hot air coming from the unit, but a fence or other cover with a number of openings for air circulation is neater and less injurious to nearby plants.

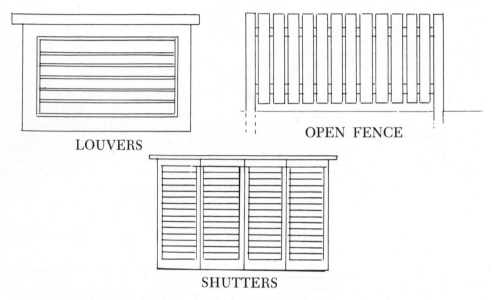

LOUVERS

OPEN FENCE

SHUTTERS

Ways to conceal an air conditioner

The oblong design of screening for the air conditioner on this patio harmonizes with the house and with the paving of marble slabs. Designed by C. M. Harrington, Jr. *Photography by Wells*

Ornamental wrought-iron sections salvaged from an old fence separate patio from woodland. *Robert Miner photo for* Home Garden

73

6

Privacy for the Patio

IF THE PATIO OR TERRACE is to be a true outdoor room it must have privacy. Then it can be as useful as any room in the house, a place for solitary relaxation, for discussions, or a jolly party. Screening out neighboring properties also helps to keep the patio in character with its own background; an Early Colonial setting will not have to compete with the Japanese style next door.

Privacy does not always require that a terrace be enclosed by a high wall or fence. Seclusion depends on various factors, such as the size of the property and the slope of the land. On a small city lot, where space is at a premium and the patio includes most of the area with tall buildings close by, a high fence or wall *is* necessary. In the country, trees and shrubs often suffice.

A high wall gives the utmost privacy but the attractive grille in the door makes it seem less forbidding. Privet and lilac bushes soften the straight line. *Photography by Wells*

This unusual screening for an air conditioner or trash can confuses the eye while allowing good circulation of air. *Photography by Wells*

A trellis at the back of this patio is covered with translucent Fiberglas panels that let in light while giving privacy. The round canvas sunshade is supported from the sides with no pole to interrupt the living space. *Canvas Awning Institute*

A screen of translucent Fiberglas is lighted from behind by floodlights which throw foliage shadows from outside onto the screen. *General Electric Co.*

FENCES AND SCREENS

Prefabricated fences come in many designs and various heights with sections ready to install. The useful stockade fence is usually made of durable cedar stakes; redwood fences are supplied in basket-weave or louvered sections. By stepping sections down, they can be made to fit slopes as well as level ground. For curved or irregular outlines there are woven-wood fences of cedar or Japanese-style bamboo-reed. These come in rolls twenty-five feet long and six feet high. Bamboo is inexpensive, and while it will not last as long as cedar, it gives good service standing up well under bad weather and snow. All woven fences must be put on a stout framework. Fences of cedar or redwood can be stained or weathered to soft gray, making a mellow background for flowers and vines.

Sheets of corrugated or plain asbestos cement make handsome screens. The corrugated surface creates an interesting texture with shadows; plain panels set off picturesque plants. Translucent plastic or Fiberglas also comes in corrugated or plain sheets. It has the advantage of admitting filtered light to plants near it. At night a spectacular effect results from back-lighting, the shrubs and vines then silhouetted against the screen.

Plastic and asbestos materials likewise come in colors, to blend with the color of the house or compose an abstract pattern of squares and rectangles. Sections of fencing interspersed with evergreens of the same height or higher make an interesting screen. For small areas, canvas tied to frames made of pipe, or a lattice of laths offers a pleasant change.

For a patio at the seashore, a high board fence is an excellent means to privacy; it also protects plants from strong sea breezes (Alice Ireys, L.A.). *Molly Adams photo*

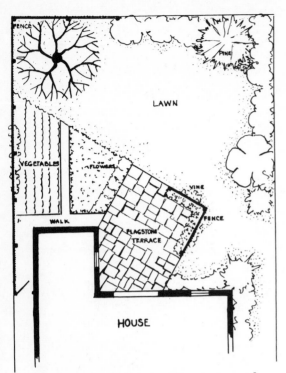

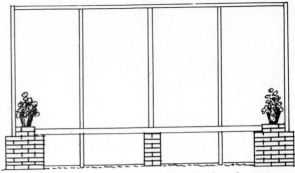

Translucent panels set in back of a planter

Row of plywood panels on stakes

Plastic panel framed by woven-reed matting

Sometimes turning a patio at an angle makes it possible to combine short sections of fence with planting to obtain the necessary privacy.

Plastic or Fiberglas panels come in four-by-eight-foot sections and in various colors that can be combined to make a screen.

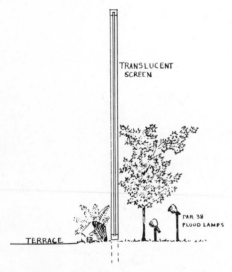

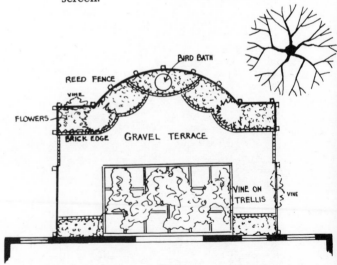

Leave room behind a translucent fence for plants. Shine a spotlight on the plants to make shadow patterns on the fence at night as shown.

In a new housing development where there are no trees, a small enclosed patio outside a picture window can provide a private place for outdoor living and an attractive view from inside. The vine on the trellis shades the window as well as the patio in hot weather.

WALLS

Walls give the greatest sense of seclusion to a terrace. Since walls are structural, it is wise to associate them with the architecture of the house—brick walls with a brick house, cement or stucco with the Spanish style, and perhaps concrete block with a modern dwelling. A partial wall extending out from the house will often give as much privacy as is needed for a suburban home, the planting at the boundary doing the rest.

Walls or fences should be attractive on both sides. Plant vines to soften the hard lines of a wall—clinging vines to make a pattern on the

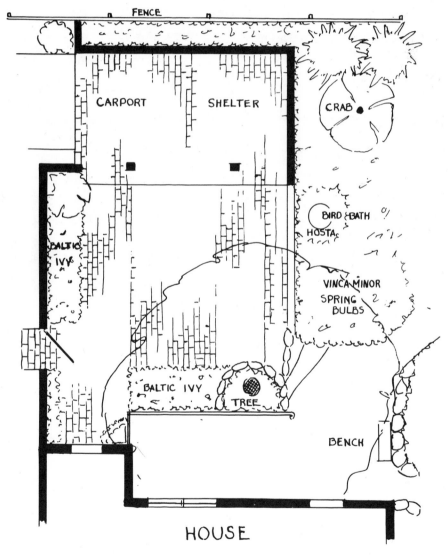

A carport, when empty, serves as a shelter adjoining the patio, as seen on page 87.

surface, often attractive in winter as well as summer, and supported vines to fall over the top in a cascade of foliage and flowers. If there is plenty of room, put a boundary fence in but at a minimum of four feet from the edge of a property, and plant flowering shrubs and trees behind it. This will add height to a four- or five-foot fence, and make a good-looking screen for the neighbors as well.

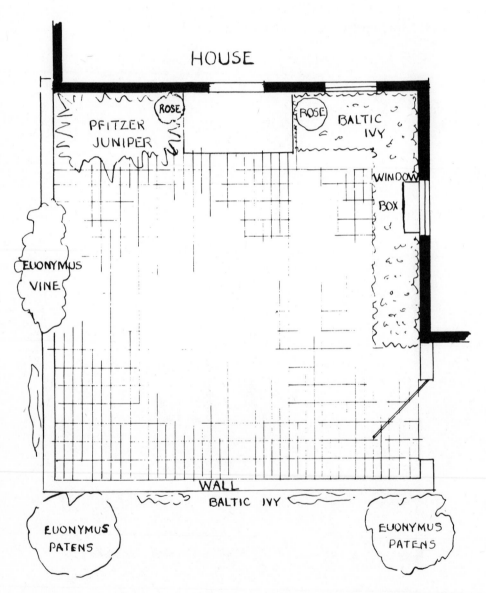

Complete privacy is provided by a wall and two sides of a house.

It takes a tall screen to conceal a house on a higher level. Here a stone retaining wall with a fence on top and the feathery foliage of Moraine locust trees combine to create privacy. *Photography by Wells*

Despite the many open spaces, decorative concrete-block walls give a high degree of privacy, especially if vines are planted to clamber over them.

HEDGES AND SLOPES

A dense hedge is an inexpensive means to privacy if there is room for the width. Privet, bush honeysuckle, lilac, and the evergreen *Euonymus patens* make a quick tall hedge. Their stems are thick enough for screening even after the leaves fall. And hedges have the advantage of looking the same on both sides.

Another interesting way of getting privacy is to build up a gently sloping ridge of earth three to five feet high along the edge of the terrace or farther out on the property. The ridge can be eight to twenty feet wide, either in a straight line or in irregular curves. Height and width will depend on the amount of available space. Cover the slopes with an informal planting of flowering shrubs, evergreens, and ground-cover. Such a screen will effectively shut out noise and gasoline fumes on the street side and make a lovely background on the terrace side for a feature, such as a pool or statue. On a smaller scale the same way of piling soil makes a grand setting for a rock garden with shrubs at the top for added height. Look at pictures of fine rock gardens to study the correct and pleasing placement of stones. Use native rock and lay it horizontally so that it will look natural and restful. Of course, a rock garden is a place to grow alpine plants and not to show off rocks. Well-chosen plants will fill in the crevices, flow gracefully over the ledges, and fill the whole area with easy-to-maintain foliage and, in spring, with sheets of interesting flowers.

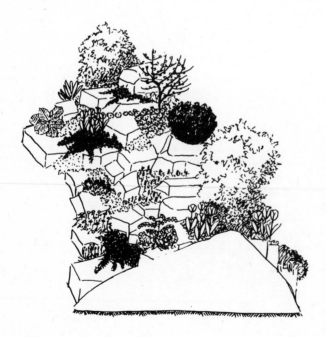

If there is no slope for a rock garden, make a mound along the edge of the terrace and enjoy growing alpine plants while you hide an unsightly view beyond.

To please a neighbor, solve the privacy problem on both sides of the property line. Plant a smoothly curving serpentine hedge with a low-branching flowering tree in each curve.

Sloping land has its special privacy problems that a fence around the terrace will not solve. Several levels of planting can be helpful. If the land slopes up from the terrace, plant at the top of the slope, using medium-sized flowering shrubs and evergreens, such as juniper and Austrian pine or hemlock to add as much height as possible. Thick low-branching trees, perhaps pin oak and hawthorn, would also be suitable. Such a high screen will keep houses beyond from looking down on the terrace.

When the land slopes down, a low planting next to the terrace, with trees far enough below for their upper branches to hide the view will solve the problem.

To get privacy next to the street either leave a mound of soil, as here, or make one for an elevated planting of trees, evergreens, and ground covers. *Speidel Studio*

7

Trees, Shrubs, and Vines for a Well-dressed Patio

THERE IS NOTHING LIKE A FINE TREE to give character and individuality to a patio. The tree, ideally, will be airy and not smothering, still providing a canopy of shade. A tree changes with the seasons—pale green or colored buds in spring, moving lights and shadows of summer leaves, autumn color, and exquisite traceries of bare branches against the winter sky.

The perfect shade for a large terrace is a tree. This terrace has been planned for easy maintenance with a hedge of *Deutzia lemoinei* and oleanders in tubs in front of the windows. *Euonymus fortunei acutus* covers the slope below the wall (Anne Bruce Haldeman, L.A.).

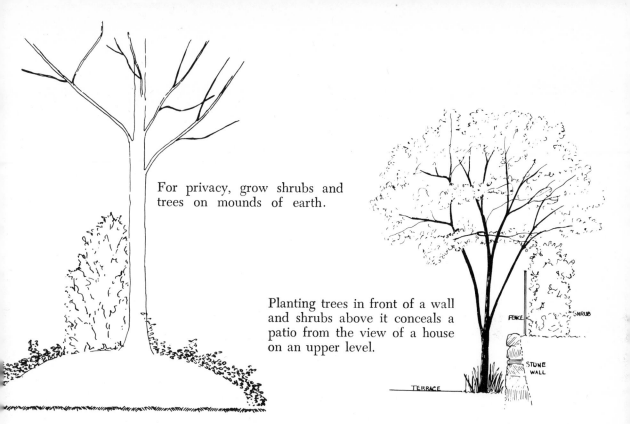

For privacy, grow shrubs and trees on mounds of earth.

Planting trees in front of a wall and shrubs above it conceals a patio from the view of a house on an upper level.

Anything of great value deserves careful selection. Check with your local nursery for the hardiness, ultimate size, and rate of growth of the tree. Don't plant such potential giants as American elm, white oak, or tulip-tree close to the house. Set any of these out from the patio about twenty feet, where they will have room to develop into superb trees, in many years, and their wide-spreading branches will overhang the patio, giving plenty of shade. And unless you are really young you will do better with more rapidly growing trees.

Large trees with close-to-the-surface, spreading roots, such as sugar maple or sycamore, can break up paving if the paving is close around the trunk. Sometimes the hungry fine surface roots of an elm near a planter or flower bed will keep flowers or shrubs from thriving. Even grass will not grow well under most maples, lindens, and a number of other trees unless the soil is frequently fed and copiously watered.

Some trees are a poor choice because they constantly drop leaves, blossoms, or fruit. Mulberry is one. The berries stain pavement and furnishings. Osage-orange litters the ground in fall with its large globes of fruit, and the sycamore sheds pieces of bark and its big leaves, a few at a time, all summer. The fluffy pink flowers of the silk-tree drop off but the tree has qualities to offset that. The seed balls of the sweet-gum are not hard to sweep up late in the fall, and so this tree might be tolerated.

Bushes and tall trees at the top of a slope screen a patio below from a house above.

A hedge at the edge and trees planted partway down a slope effectively screen a patio from a house below.

LARGE SHADE TREES FOR THE PATIO

Hackberry	*Celtis occidentalis*
Japanese pagoda-tree	*Sophora japonica*
Little-leaf linden	*Tilia cordata*
Red maple	*Acer rubrum*
Red oak	*Quercus rubra*
River birch	*Betula nigra*
Sweetgum	*Liquidambar styraciflua*
Thornless honey-locust	*Gleditsia triacanthos inermis*
Tulip-tree	*Liriodendron tulipifera*
Yellowwood	*Cladrastis lutea*
Zelkova	*Zelkova serrata*

FLOWERING TREES

Many flowering trees are not big enough to give much shade, but the smaller ones are decorative as accents or grown against a large expanse of bare wall. You can also plant them in the shubbery border or in front of evergreens. Scent can be pleasing or unpleasant. The perfume of a fringe-tree on a spring morning or of linden on an early-summer day is a delight. On the other hand, the strong odor of the tree lilac is obnoxious if close by, and also that of hawthorn to many people. Fortunately most flowering trees do not have a strong fragrance.

Cornelian-cherry	*Cornus mas*	yellow	25 feet
Crape-myrtle	*Lagerstroemia indica*	pink, red, white, purple	20 feet
Empress-tree	*Paulownia tomentosa*	purple	40 feet
Flowering cherry	*Prunus* in variety	pink, white	20 feet
Flowering crabapple	*Malus* in variety	pink, white	8–40 feet
Flowering dogwood	*Cornus florida*	white, pink	40 feet
Franklin-tree	*Franklinia alatamaha*	white	30 feet
Fringe-tree	*Chionanthus virginica*	white	15 feet
Goldenchain-tree	*Laburnum vossi*	yellow	15 feet
Goldenrain-tree	*Koelreuteria paniculata*	yellow	30 feet
Japanese dogwood	*Cornus kousa*	white	20 feet
Japanese pagoda-tree	*Sophora japonica*	yellow-white	75 feet
Japanese snowbell *	*Styrax japonica*	white	30 feet
Mountain-ash	*Sorbus americana*	white	20 feet
Redbud	*Cercis canadensis*	magenta, white	25 feet
Saucer magnolia	*Magnolia soulangeana*	pink	25 feet
Shadbush	*Amelanchier canadensis*	pale pink	20 feet
Silk-tree	*Albizzia julibrissin*	pink	25 feet
Silver-bell-tree	*Halesia carolina*	white	30 feet
Smoke-tree	*Cotinus coggygria*	gray-pink	15 feet
Stewartia	*Stewartia ovata grandiflora*	white	15 feet
Washington thorn	*Crataegus phaenopyrum*	white	20 feet

* Not reliably hardy north of Washington, D.C.

The wall of this patio connects house and carport making a continuous line which is structurally pleasing. When the car is out, the carport doubles as a shelter and enlarges the patio for a party. *Photography by Wells*

MULTIPLE-STEMMED AND LOW-BRANCHING TREES

A tree can be useful not only for shade, but for its beauty of form and foliage. Multiple-stemmed trees provide a wide area of shade and also make an attractive pattern seen at eye-level. A row of them can make a partial screen or divider, or a decoration against a building. Some trees branch so low that they have the same effect as those with multiple stems. Select properly shaped plants right at the nursery. Some trees can also be trained flat against a wall as espaliers and are very effective used this way.

Birch	*Betula* in variety
Crape-myrtle *	*Lagerstroemia indica*
Franklin-tree	*Franklinia alatamaha*
Redbud	*Cercis canadensis*
Saucer magnolia	*Magnolia soulangeana*
Shadbush	*Amelanchier canadensis*
Silk-tree	*Albizzia julibrissin*
Smoke-tree	*Cotinus coggygria*
Staghorn sumac	*Rhus hirta*
Yellowwood	*Cladrastis lutea*

* Not hardy north of Virginia.

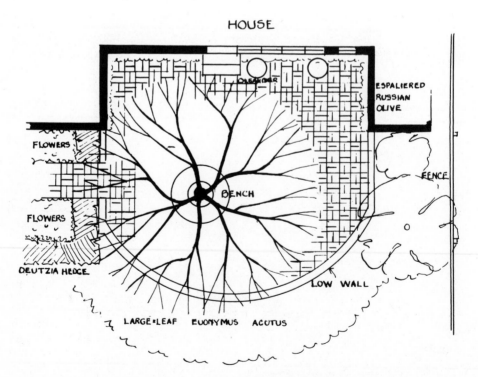

This patio was built around a large elm. Brick laid in sand allows plenty of moisture to reach the tree.

In the broad terrace in sun and shade at the back of the inn, trees and shrubs flourish in adequate openings in the paving. Unless paving is laid in sand without mortar, plenty of space must always be allowed for roots to receive moisture and air. *Colonial Williamsburg photo*

In a woodland setting, clumps of birch and rhododendron form a natural background for an informal little patio. The brick paths delineate planting beds for ground covers, bulbs, and perennials. *Molly Adams photo*

A wide-spreading tree with low-forking branches is a point of interest on this Japanese-style terrace with paving of concrete squares laid in pebbles. *George Taloumis photo*

A tree, trimmed in the shape of a parasol, shades a stone-in-grass patio. *George Taloumis photo*

A wide brick path bordered by flowers leads to a tree-shaded dining patio beside the kitchen door. *Molly Adams photo*

It is not healthy to expose the roots of a tree or to cover them with more than a few inches of soil. If there is a tree on sloping ground where the patio is to go, either build (*left*) a retaining wall around the tree or (*right*) make a pit for it.

COLUMNAR TREES

Where space is limited, as it is in an atrium, a tall narrow tree is best. There are a number of kinds of columnar trees. Some of them produce flowers.

Cherry 'Milky Way'	*Prunus serrulata amanogawa 'Milky Way'*
Crabapple 'Van Eseltine'	*Malus 'Van Eseltine'*
Doric maple	*Acer rubrum columnare 'Doric'*
Gray birch	*Betula populifolia*
Hawthorn	*Crataegus monogyna stricta*
Hornbeam	*Carpinus betulus pyramidalis*
Red oak	*Quercus robur fastigiata*
Sentry gingko	*Gingko biloba fastigiata*
Wilson's mountain-ash	*Sorbus aucuparia wilsoni*

Trees that normally have low-spreading or pendent branches, such as pin oak or weeping willow, are a poor choice for the patio; they take up too much room. Consider all these characteristics when selecting trees if you do not luckily have one already standing in the right place.

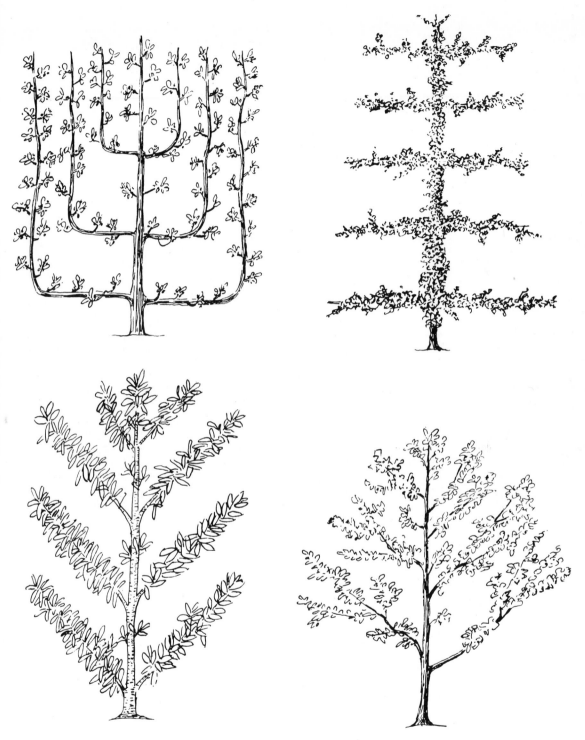

Small trees and shrubs can be espaliered against a wall in various formal designs or allowed to branch naturally.

Shrubs

Once properly planted and in the right soil, shrubs are the most easy-to-care-for plants. This ease of cultivation plus their summer-long verdure and their various periods of showy bloom make them most desirable on the patio margins. They soften the solid look of paving; they can be the major contributor of life and of green. Evergreen shrubs—rhododendrons, azaleas, yew, mountain-laurel, and others—make the best basic planting. Combine them to utilize their variety of textures. Try the somber dark green of yews with the bright green of hollies. Oregon-grape, leucothoe, and abelia have bronze or purple tints in winter that contrast well with the feathery green of Pfitzer junipers. In climates where broad-leaved evergreens need protection, plant them on the north side of the house or a high wall where sun will not burn the leaves in a winter drought.

Certain twig formations furnish variety in winter so plant some deciduous shrubs with the evergreens to avoid monotony. The scarlet of red-twigged dogwood gleams against winter snow. Pale gray lilac branches make a strong pattern against a dark wall. These are simply suggestions. To make proper selection, do visit a nursery, study the plants there, and discuss with the nurseryman their behavior in your climate.

Beds of annuals in front of a white fence in the corner of a flagstone terrace include petunias, dahlias, cleome, marguerites, and an edging of sweet-alyssum. *George Taloumis photo*

EVERGREENS

Azalea	*Azalea* in variety
Boxwood, dwarf	*Buxus sempervirens suffruticosa*
Boxwood, Korean	*B. microphylla koreana*
Evergreen euonymus	*Euonymus* in variety
Firethorn (sometimes deciduous)	*Pyracantha coccinea lalandi*
Holly	*Ilex* in variety
Japanese andromeda	*Pieris japonica*
Juniper, Pfitzer	*Juniperus pfitzeriana compacta*
Juniper, procumbent	*J. procumbens*
Leucothoe	*Leucothoe catesbaei*
Mugho pine	*Pinus mugo mughus*
Oregon-grape	*Mahonia aquifolium*
Rhododendron	*Rhododendron* in variety
Yew	*Taxus* in variety

DECIDUOUS SHRUBS

Abelia	*Abelia grandiflora*
Azalea	*Azalea* in variety
Barberry	*Berberis thunbergi*
Cotoneaster, cranberry	*Cotoneaster apiculata*
Dwarf blueberry-bush	*Viburnum opulus nanum*
Flowering-quince	*Chaenomeles lagenaria*
Fragrant snowball	*Viburnum carlesi*
Maries viburnum	*V. tomentosum mariesi*
Nandina *	*Nandina domestica*
Privet, Chinese	*Ligustrum sinense*
Privet, Regel's	*L. obtusifolium regelianum*
Red-twigged dogwood	*Cornus stolenifera*
Slender deutzia	*Deutzia gracilis*
Spirea 'Anthony Waterer'	*Spirea bumalda* 'Anthony Waterer'
Winged euonymus	*Euonymus alatus*

* Not reliably hardy north of Washington, D.C.

CLIMATE CONTROL

Besides being beautiful, shrubs on a patio affect the temperature. They absorb heat and do not reflect it back the way paving does. Shrubs planted between patio and house keep both house and paving cooler on hot days. Areas of green set in the pavement also have a cooling effect.

BERRIED PLANTS TO ATTRACT BIRDS

One of the many pleasures of outdoor living is bird watching. You can lure many more birds to your patio if you plant shrubs and trees nearby for food and nesting. The bright berries that attract birds also add to the beauty of the garden. Some berries, as those of the mountain-ash, are devoured as soon as they ripen, but the firethorn keeps its clusters of orange fruit till late in the winter when birds are really hungry. In summer, hummingbirds come to certain bushes with trumpet blossoms, like those of abelias.

Arrow-wood	*Viburnum dentatum*
Black-alder	*Ilex verticillata*
Bush honeysuckle	*Lonicera tatarica*
Carmine crabapple	*Malus atrosanguinea*
Cornelian-cherry	*Cornus mas*
Cranberry-bush	*Viburnum opulus*
Firethorn	*Pyracantha coccinea lalandi*
Flowering dogwood	*Cornus florida*
Highbush blueberry	*Vaccinium corymbosum*
Inkberry	*Ilex glabra*
Japanese barberry	*Berberis thunbergi*
Japanese flowering crabapple	*Malus floribunda*
Mountain-ash	*Sorbus americana*
Nannyberry	*Viburnum lentago*
Red-cedar	*Juniperus virginiana*
Regel's privet	*Ligustrum obtusifolium regelianum*
Shadbush	*Amelanchier canadensis*
Washington thorn	*Crataegus phaenopyrum*

In a break in the Japanese-holly hedge a dogwood is espaliered in a natural style against a plain wall. *George Taloumis photo*

A flowering crabapple espaliered against a house wall makes a background for a fountain. Designed by C. M. Harrington, Jr. *Photography by Wells*

Beds of iris along a wide flagstone walk make an attractive approach for a patio at a distance from the house. *Schreiner's Gardens photo*

Two shaded patios with brick walls and brick floors.
Above, designed by owner; *below,* designed by Gay
McDonnell. *Photography by Wells*

Two views of a patio with a fountain figure and beds of flowers along the outside. Design by author. *Photography by Wells*

Above, night lighting extends the livability of a patio. *General Electric Co. photo. Below,* decorated with great pots of roses, a deck in San Francisco overlooks a distant view (Jackson & Perkins Co.). *George de Gennaro photo*

The Dependable Vines

Vines are a boon to patios. They require little ground space, cover a large area in a short time with beautiful foliage, and afford the same privacy as an established hedge. On an arbor or high trellis they can give shade. Many also have colorful flowers. You can train some vines into various designs or shapes. Probably no plants require so little care or have so few pests. But it is important to choose the right vine for each situation, otherwise a rampant grower may get out of control or a delicate vine fail to give the luxuriance you expected.

Some vines climb by twining and require wire, string, or trellis for support. Don't plant a twining vine against a tree; it may in time strangle the tree. Select a vigorous grower like wisteria only if you can provide a very strong support, give plenty of room, and have time to prune it regularly.

A multiple-stemmed fringe-tree (*Chionanthus virginica*) pruned high gives light shade for the dooryard terrace where Helen Van Pelt Wilson's many house plants spend the summer. *Molly Adams photo*

TWINING VINES

Actinidia	*Actinidia* species
Bittersweet	*Celastrus scandens*
Dutchman's-pipe	*Aristolochia durior*
Everblooming honeysuckle	*Lonicera heckrotti*
Five-leaf akebia	*Akebia quinata*
Kadsura *	*Kadsura japonica*
Morning-glory	*Ipomoea*
Silver-lace-vine	*Polygonum auberti*
Wisteria	*Wisteria* species

TENDRIL VINES

Clematis	*Clematis* species and varieties
Cup-and-saucer-vine	*Cobaea scandens*
Grape	*Vitis* species and varieties
Passion-flower *	*Passiflora* species
Virginia-creeper	*Parthenocissus quinquefolia*

CLINGING VINES

These vines have rootlike holdfasts or suction disks that stick to surfaces. They are good on walls and on trees, but not where they can dislodge wood.

Boston ivy	*Parthenocissus tricuspidata*
Creeping fig *	*Ficus pumila*
Climbing hydrangea	*Hydrangea petiolaris*
English ivy	*Hedera helix*
Trumpet-creeper	*Campsis radicans*
Winter-creeper	*Euonymus fortunei*

* Hardy only in the South.

8

Flowers for Color

COMPLETE ENJOYMENT OF FLOWERS depends on seeing them at close range, so concentrate your flowers on or close by your patio. Flowers have an affinity for brick and flagstone and paving sets them off. Either a permanent flower bed or a grouping of plants in containers brightens the whole patio.

Colorful annuals brighten this hospitable, sunny, brick-paved patio with a fountain figure in the center. Designed by author. *Photography by Wells*

Start the display with a sizable drift of color from spring bulbs. They are most rewarding for the little trouble involved in planting them, and need little care after blooming other than to let their leaves ripen and yellow. Little crocuses will open at the base of a tree on warm days even in late winter or thrust their cheerful purple, white, or yellow cups up through the ground-cover along the edge of the paving. Tulips lend themselves to formal array or to groupings with creeping phlox and snow-white hardy candytuft. An attractive natural grouping could be narcissus with forget-me-nots and grape hyacinths. If there is a retaining wall, let sunshiny basket-of-gold alyssum spill over the edge.

Bamboo, ferns, English ivy and a privet hedge all do well in the shady sheltered corner of this brick-paved patio. *Photography by Wells*

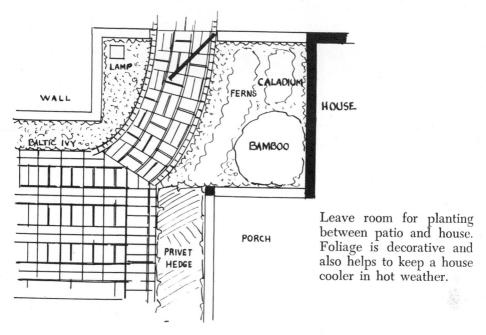

Leave room for planting between patio and house. Foliage is decorative and also helps to keep a house cooler in hot weather.

On a sunny patio, floribunda roses in rich colors parade all summer, and annual bedding plants—petunias, geraniums, marigolds, and dwarf snapdragons—bloom for a long season. These are easily procured as started plants at wayside stands and garden centers. In the fall the rich colors of chrysanthemums take over. Use your imagination to develop a lively or a subtle color scheme to suit your taste.

Large flagstones make a good floor for this patio, which is conveniently close to the porch door. *Molly Adams photo*

Container Gardening

Add warmth, charm, and accent to your patio with plants in containers. These give enchanting effects, are practical, and can be moved. You can have vibrant color in the shade, particularly with impatiens in several new varieties, or dramatize a doorway, steps, or a fountain with a planned display on festive occasions. Potted plants are not hard to keep at the peak of perfection.

The variety of forms and sizes of containers is fascinating. There are garlanded terra-cotta or marble urns, old-fashioned strawberry jars, redwood planters in various shapes, painted tubs or boxes, metal basins

Where there is little room for planting between house and patio, vines add softening foliage and flowers to cover large wall spaces. Here roses and wisteria are trained on wires against the walls. *Healy photo*

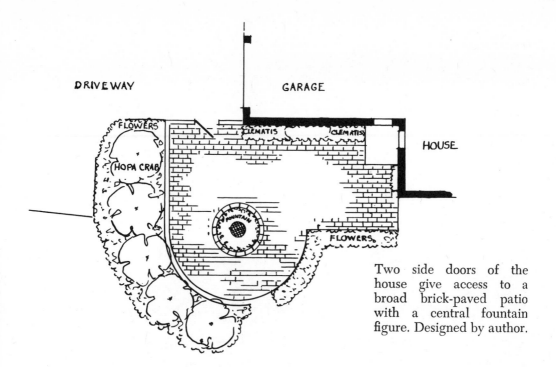

DRIVEWAY GARAGE

CLEMATIS CLEMATIS

FLOWERS

HOPA CRAB

FOUNTAIN

FLOWERS

HOUSE

Two side doors of the house give access to a broad brick-paved patio with a central fountain figure. Designed by author.

shallow or deep, as well as the familiar but always appropriate clay flower pots. You can contrive unusual containers out of driftwood, old iron and copper kettles, washtubs, or flue tiles. Perch them on platforms, set them in rows on wall shelves, or hang them from brackets. Set containers wherever an accent or color is needed.

A fuchsia in a hanging pot on a brick wall shows to advantage and brightens an otherwise bare area. *George Taloumis photo*

103

The late-summer fragrant-flowering silver-lace-vine (*Polygonum auberti*), instead of running riot over the stockade fence, is trained to a rectangular wire framework and kept clipped. At the base a narrow bed of lily-turf (*Liriope spicata*) is edged with brick interspersed with stones.

Distinctive or handsome containers will add character to a garden. Collecting them can become an absorbing pastime. Anything with simple lines to make a quiet foil for the flowers will do, but it must be large enough for an adequate amount of soil and have a drainage hole. To

104

plant, first cover the bottom with an inch or more of coarse gravel, and then use a mixture of soil, sand, and peat moss.

Choose plants which have interesting and enduring foliage as well as a long season of bloom. If you limit yourself to one kind, you can start new plants or tubers in successive weeks to prolong the display.

Ageratum	Daisies	Lantanas
Azaleas	Dwarf cannas	Marigolds
Baltic ivy	Ferns	Petunias
Begonias, fibrous-rooted	Fuchsias	Primroses
Begonias, tuberous	Geraniums	Salvias
Caladiums	Hyacinths	Succulents
Cinerarias	Hybrid lilies	of all kinds
Cyclamens	Hydrangeas	Tulips

Overlooking a large formal garden, this flagstone patio is also suitably elegant with a handsome iron fence, tubs of blue hydrangeas, and standards of clipped box (Annette Hoyt Flanders, L.A.). *Mattie Edwards Hewitt photo*

Leave a free-form island in the pavement for a planting of ground cover, bulbs, low perennials, and an evergreen for accent.

To Dramatize Patio Plants

Leave an island in the paving for a colorful display of flowers and evergreens, using plants of different heights, but all fairly low, to make an interesting pattern. An open place for planting can be free-form or geometrical. You can work out intriguing designs with planted squares, triangles, and circles in the paving, using bands of flowers in solid colors. But be sure to leave plenty of room also for seating arrangements.

Show off flowers in a raised bed. One with a bench along the edge is doubly nice. Make a feature of topiary work by setting a sculptured evergreen on a stand, or emphasizing it with a square or circle of colored gravel.

Waterlilies thrive in containers in a sunny pool. Tubs or boxes ten to twelve inches across and as deep, sunk so that there is six inches of water over the top, provide ideal growing conditions for them. The large waxy flowers of tropical waterlilies are lusciously colored, easy to grow, and once started need neither watering nor weeding.

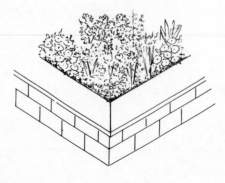

A raised bed on a patio is a good place to display flowers, and if the edging is wide, it can serve for seating.

106

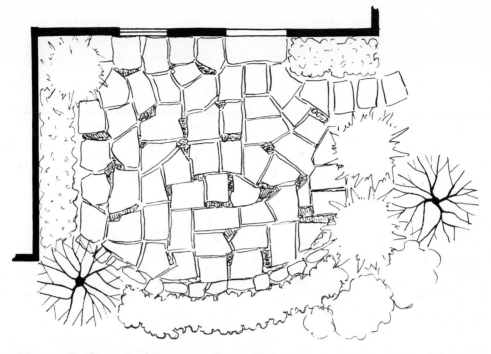

Although flagstones laid for pavement gardening are usually irregular, as far as possible make the lines parallel so the design will have a restful effect. Leave plenty of spaces for planting.

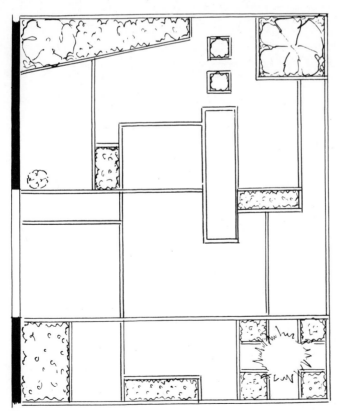

Divide paving into sections with redwood spacers leaving small open areas for plants. Save room for seating arrangements.

107

Under a dramatically leaning oak tree, broad bands of bishop's-weed (*Aegopodium podagraria*) edge a wide brick walk leading to a small patio in a woodland setting. This is a good ground cover for difficult places where it can spread without becoming a nuisance. *Photography by Wells*

Pavement Gardening with Crevice Plants

Pavement gardening is a charming way to get plants on a terrace. Green leaves and tiny bright flowers show up like jewels against the paving. Leave spaces between bricks or irregular flagstones and set in some plants. Put stone chips around the plants as a mulch if there is room. Fill every available crack and crevice. Tuck in larger plants around the edge of the patio. Thyme and a few other plants do not mind being stepped on. Ajuga is also rugged.

Ajuga	Ice-plant
Alpine dianthus	Santolina
Campanula carpatica	Sedums
Creeping phlox	Sempervivums
Dwarf snapdragons	Thyme
Heathers	

Fragrant Plants, and Lights for Flowers

To come out onto patio or terrace and get a whiff of fragrance is delightful. Remember the powerful scent of lilac and mock-orange, the heady perfume of hyacinths. In lightly shaded corners where little else will grow, the sweet bells of lily-of-the-valley open among the slender green leaves. Many roses are marvelously fragrant, as 'Crimson Glory', 'Chrysler Imperial', and 'Pink Peace'. Some of the old bush roses, cabbage or moss, are also quite fragrant. Trumpets of regal and auratum lilies perfume the summer air.

For scented edgings, plant sweet-alyssum or mignonette. Some of the aromatic herbs also make nice border plants. Silver or green santolinas are spicy; grayish-leaved lavender is refreshing.

Many flowers are especially fragrant at night, and can greatly increase one's enjoyment of the patio in the evening. Most nocturnal flowers are white or pale colored and gleam in the moonlight as they perfume the air.

Tuberoses are strongly perfumed both day and night. The fragrance of nicotiana, or tobacco plant, is intensified as the two-inch tubular flowers open at dusk. This is an annual easily grown in either sun or part shade. Sweet-rocket, whose botanical name *Hesperis* means evening, is sweeter scented when it opens at night. It blooms at the same time as iris and once planted, seeds itself. The aromatic gas-plant (*Dictamnus*) has racemes of pink or white flowers which give off a resinous gas. On a windless night, you can ignite the gas without harming the flowers.

To add an interesting effect to the patio at night, one can place lights among the flowers. White lights are best for showing up their colors. Soft reflecting lights can be set on pointed metal stakes and shifted about as plantings change through the seasons. Lighting the flowers also increases pleasure in the garden around the patio.

Electric lights skillfully placed in a flower border make possible full enjoyment of a garden at night. *General Electric Co.*

9

Ground-covers and Mulches
for Easy Maintenance

TODAY'S GARDEN PLANS emphasize low maintenance, and on a patio this is most needful. You cannot feel relaxed or in a mood for entertaining with garden work staring you in the face. Two great work- and time-savers are ground-covers and mulches. Ground-covers are delightful plants which, once established, clothe the soil so densely that there is no room for weeds. If you plant ground-covers under shrubs, they conserve moisture in the soil, and many will grow under trees where nothing else can compete with the roots. In poor soil and in those narrow bands next to the foundation of a house they will flourish. They are indispensable for stopping erosion on slopes. Ground-covers make a neat finish to a patio planting and help to keep soil from splashing onto paving when it rains. Most ground-covers can be clipped.

One way to have plants on a formal patio is to interrupt the paving with a pattern of small formal beds. Outlined in brick and edged with dwarf boxwood, these beds are filled with geraniums. *George Taloumis photo*

Ground-covers with Flowers

If the ground out from the patio slopes up or down, plant the bank with rampant winter-creepers, *Euonymus fortunei* or *E. f. coloratus*, with purplish leaves. The trailing white *Rosa wichuraiana* and the pink 'Max Graf' make fine flowering ground-covers. Crown-vetch (*Coronilla varia*) produces a wealth of pink bloom, stands dry weather well, and grows well on steep banks.

Gray-green leaves on plants are usually a sign of drought-resistance. The woolly yarrow (*Achillea tomentosa*) will grow even between paving stones, and its yellow flowers harmonize with day-lilies for a care-free colorful border. Leadwort (*Plumbago larpentiae*), which starts blooming in late summer and goes on till frost, offers vivid cobalt blue for a terrace. Creeping phlox (*Phlox subulata*) in pink, white, or lavender, makes a flowing carpet of color in spring, and bulbs can come up through it. Later the little rose or white flowers of the sand pink (*Dianthus deltoides*) rise above their gray-green cushions.

Sweet-scented thyme and red-centered white pinks thrive in crevices left between the stones. *George Taloumis photo*

GROUND-COVERS WITHOUT FLOWERS

Ground-covers without noticeable flowers are also attractive as well as useful. Succulents of many kinds cover the ground with various sculptured forms, green and reddish green. The green upright spirals of pachysandra (*Pachysandra terminalis*) grow in dense shade. Where a large area is to be planted some of the prostrate junipers as the form 'Andorra' (*Juniperus horizontalis plumosa*) and the Japanese garden juniper (*Juniperus procumbens*) fill in more quickly than do smaller plants. The dark green, well-shaped leaves of Baltic ivy (*Hedera helix baltica*) are always a pleasing sight.

The qualifications for a good ground-cover are the ability to spread rapidly and the continuous production of attractive year-round foliage. Flowers are a bonus. Some ground-covers like pachysandra do well in dense shade, others like woolly yarrow on hot, dry, rocky ground.

A ground cover of pachysandra helps to relate the patio to the shrub planting along the sides and to the fence and benches.

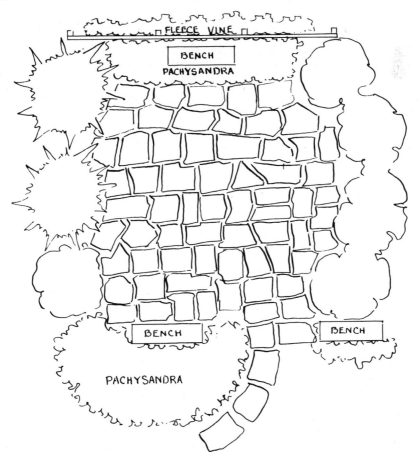

113

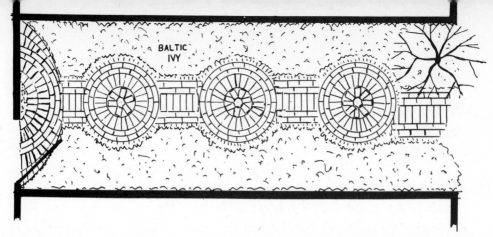

Circular sections of brick paving in the walk are surrounded by ivy and make the narrow space seem wider.

Set out plants in rows about twelve to fifteen inches apart for easy cultivation the first year. Depending on the plant, it takes two to three years to get a dense cover. Some kinds like the hardy myrtle root wherever a branch touches soil: others like the favorite ajuga send out runners from the center in the way of strawberries. Some, like pachysandra, increase by underground roots. Don't plant ground-covers in a perennial border; they will usually choke out other plants. It is easy to keep ground-covers clipped in neat designs or to contain them with paving.

A Selection of Plants

Baltic ivy	*Hedera helix baltica*	Shade
Carpet bugle	*Ajuga reptans*	Shade
Creeping phlox	*Phlox subulata*	Sun
Creeping veronica	*Veronica repens*	Sun
Epimedium	*Epimedium alpinum*	Shade
Golden-moss	*Sedum acre*	Sun
Japanese spurge	*Pachysandra terminalis*	Shade
Leadwort	*Plumbago larpentiae*	Sun
Lily-turf	*Liriope spicata*	Sun
Maiden pink	*Dianthus deltoides*	Sun
Myrtle or periwinkle	*Vinca minor*	Shade
Prostrate junipers	*Juniperus* species	Sun
Purple-leaf winter-creeper	*Euonymous fortunei coloratus*	Sun
Pussytoes	*Antennaria dioica rosea*	Sun
Sand pink	*Dianthus arenarius*	Sun
Snow-in-summer	*Cerastium tomentosum*	Sun
Violets	*Viola* species	Sun
Winter-creeper	*Eunoymus fortunei*	Sun
Woolly yarrow	*Achillea tomentosa*	Sun

Leading to a patio at the back of the house is this very shady walk between buildings. Ivy surrounds the decorative brick paving, strongly outlining a curved design. The vine growing to the top of the foundation wall gives height without reducing the limited planting space. *Johnston photo*

Railroad ties split in half lengthwise and across make a solid edging suitable for a terrace where the paving is made of large marble slabs. The ties are sunk two feet into the ground. A ground cover of myrtle grows around the dogwood tree and trails over the severe tops of the ties. Designed by C. M. Harrington, Jr. *Photography by Wells*

A ground cover of pachysandra is tall enough to make a nice transition between fence and flagstones, and lawn and flagstones. *George Taloumis photo*

Mulches Are Useful

Mulches are another means of keeping beds or open spaces tidy and trim. A good mulch makes a weedproof barrier that holds moisture in the soil. Choose one that is light enough to let rain seep through, and pile it lightly two to four inches thick on flower beds, shrubbery borders, and around trees. Peatmoss, ground corncobs, buckwheat hulls, shredded bark, pulverized nutshells, and partially decayed sawdust are all good.

Gravel makes an excellent mulch. It is obtainable in various sizes, in natural color, or with vinyl colors sprayed on. You can work out interesting designs with colored gravels accented with plants. Mulches, especially gravel, need an edging to keep them in place. A firm edging also holds in water.

Select an edging to suit the design of the patio. Brick laid on end is pleasing with brick paving, unless the plan is quite casual, then redwood or railroad ties would be better. Concrete bricks come in gray that blends with crushed rock. Concrete blocks are a match for a cement patio. Wood would warm it up.

Both mulches and ground-covers are a help to container gardening. Set pots on a bed of gravel and the moisture underneath will do them good. Potted house plants set down in the ground-cover for the summer will thrive there.

Sections of log set on end in the ground hold back a gravel mulch, and a chemical grass-and-weed killer sprayed along the outside makes grass trimming there unnecessary. *Photography by Wells*

Imaginative edgings with ground covers or gravel: 1. In the North, where snow covers the patio in winter, plant annuals—dwarf marigolds, petunias, or ageratum in the holes of the concrete blocks. 2. Round forms of hen-and-chickens contrast with the points on the design of redwood strips. 3. Gravel or creeping phlox is surrounded by rocks of various sizes. 4. Ivy is clipped to keep it in neat squares with a dwarf evergreen at intervals for accent.

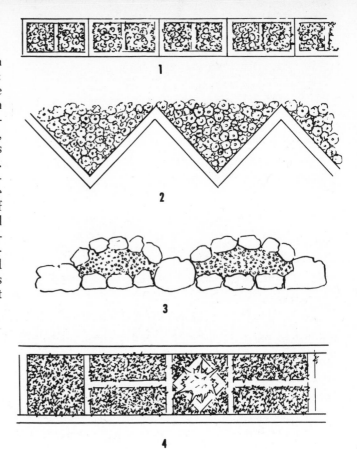

Entered through a wrought-iron gate, this secluded brick patio is well designed and wisely planted; it makes a charming setting for an outdoor dinner party. *Roche photo*

A lamp and kerosene torches give plenty of light for supper on the small upper level of this patio. Easy steps go down to a larger area. *Molly Adams photo*

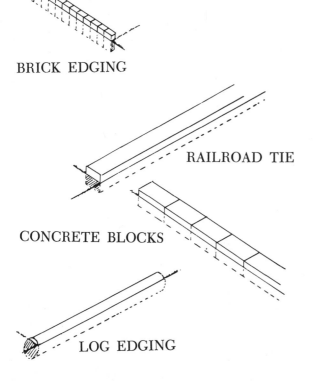

BRICK EDGING

RAILROAD TIE

CONCRETE BLOCKS

LOG EDGING

Slightly raised edgings, partly buried in the ground, keep mulches from spilling over onto the patio.

119

10

Making the Patio Livable

TO BE LIVABLE, a patio should be furnished for comfort, equipped for the activities of the family, and decorated for interest and beauty. A place for storage is essential.

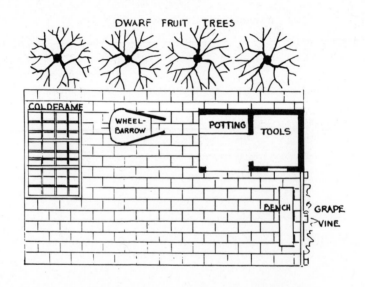

This patio is planned with storage for gardening tools, a bench for potting, coldframes, and a place to sit.

Cupboards for storage units should harmonize with the patio design. If there is a fence along one side, you can build closets in back of it, cutting doors into the fence itself, then when the doors are shut, they are not noticeable. There should be space in the closets for garden furniture and cushions, toys, brooms, rakes, and a hose.

Or you can build storage units against the house under the eaves. You can make a small cupboard to conceal the electric meter and the hose and water connections or a larger unit to hold equipment for outdoor hobbies, flower-arranging supplies, or bird food. A wooden bench with a lid can provide both extra seating and a place to store cushions and games.

The gardener will find useful a potting shed and a storage area for fertilizer, flower pots, potting soil, and hand tools. Storage units built out from the back door and under a roof would make a covered passageway to the patio.

If you build a permanent brick or stone barbecue on the patio, include space next to it for cupboards to hold outdoor dishes, cooking equipment, and fuel. Line the cupboards with metal to keep out insects and mice. The extra level space on top next to the grill will be a handy place for preparing and serving food.

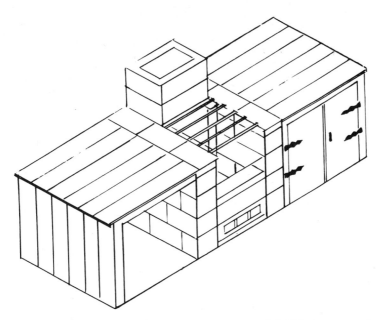

A permanent barbecue fireplace is more useful if it incorporates a cupboard for cooking equipment and a place for wood.

Outdoor cooking on the patio is fun if the chef has the proper paraphernalia at hand. *Photography by Wells*

ELECTRIC CONVENIENCES

Outside electric wiring and waterproof outlets are indispensable on the patio. Plan carefully for adequate wiring, and while the patio is being built it is easy to run wires under the paving. Lights at night are not only convenient but beautiful. They turn the surrounding area into a wonderland. Focus a light on a beautiful tree; run a line of reflecting lights through the flower border. If there are steps, light them for safety. Use white lights to show up colors, and hide the fixtures in foliage. The sources of light should not be obvious. Keep the lighting subtle and place the lights so that you will not look directly at them. Fixtures are available for down-lights, up-lights, accent light to emphasize a feature, path lights, and so on. There are special plastic-coated, all-weather bulbs in outdoor fixtures. For the patio itself there are handsome wrought-iron lanterns, ceramic globes, paper lanterns, torches, and hurricane glasses for candles.

Electricity also runs the circulating pump for a fountain or waterfall. Put in an outlet for a record player or a fan for hot evenings. If you don't want to cook on a barbecue, electric skillets and percolators are just the thing for outdoors. There are also gas grills and soft gas lights in fixtures designed like those used on long-ago city streets. Antique gas lamps can still be found by collectors.

122

At the base of a big tree a round terrazzo receptor—the type commonly used as a wash fountain in factories—serves as a garden pool. Water plants grow in submerged pots (Burks and Landberg, architects).

LIGHTS FOR FLOWER BORDERS

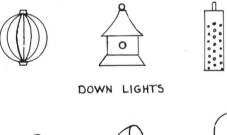

DOWN LIGHTS

FLOODLIGHTS

Illumination for the patio

Electricity can be counted on to get rid of insects. Traps with black, ultraviolet, and green lights lure and kill mosquitoes and other bothersome night insects; yellow light will not attract them. Spraying the patio also keeps away insects. Or you can put up a martin house and let the birds deal effectively with the mosquitoes.

Light makes a patio livable in the evening. Here a floodlight accents a tree, and a down-reflecting light shows off chrysanthemums in a planter. *General Electric Co.*

124

WATER

Few features of a patio give as much pleasure and beauty as a pool or water in some way, and water is easy to provide. You can have a restful mirror pool reflecting sun and shadow, the music of a running stream or waterfall, or the lively sparkle and dance of a fountain.

For reflection, you need a shallow pool just a few inches deep, and can have one made of galvanized sheet metal in any shape you like. Coat it underneath with asphalt, and paint the inside blue or black. If your pool is large, that is more than four feet across, put a drain and plug in the bottom. You can also make small reflecting pools of sheet lead.

Readymade pools of Fiberglas come in various shapes and sizes. They are easy to install. Be sure the design and materials harmonize with the patio. Pools can be constructed of native rock, brick, concrete, or plastic.

If the patio is quite small, you might like one of the little fountains now on the market with a figure and a shell-shaped pool, or a wall fountain with a semicircular catch basin below. Small submersible pumps keep water circulating as long as power is turned on. Such pools can be filled from the garden hose and emptied with a siphon. Water needs to be replaced at intervals because of evaporation.

Ground sloping down to the patio gives you a chance for a waterfall. Here again the smallest circulating pump, about as big as your fist, can lift one hundred gallons of water an hour to a height of five feet. Larger pumps will lift more water higher.

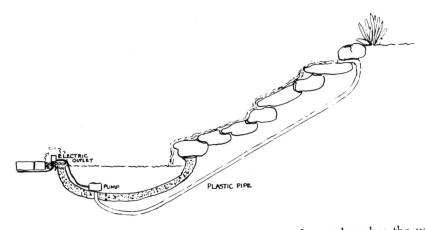

In this waterfall construction, a circulating pump in the pool pushes the water up to the top of the hill. The water splashes over flat rocks placed along the course.

125

In a small informal patio garden covered with myrtle, a water feature composed of three four-foot pools of sheet metal can be viewed from three different angles. Designed by author. *Hansbrough photo*

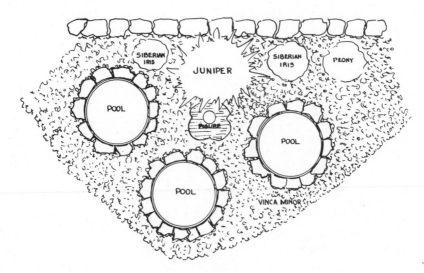

Four-foot circular pools are easily made of galvanized metal, here set in a bed of *Vinca minor*. The pools can be seen from various angles, and each one appears to be placed in front of the figure. Photograph directly above.

126

Lightweight Featherock makes fine natural-looking boulders for a waterfall on a rooftop patio. *Featherock, Inc.*

In making a waterfall, let the water drop over the edge of a rock or some straight edge and at several points on the way down. This arrangement makes a more musical sound. Or to get the splashing sound repeated, install a fountain with several catch basins at different levels. Small amounts of water can be made to sound abundant.

There are inexpensive fountain units also powered by electric motors, fountain heads for simple sprays, and rotating heads that make water fall in interlacing patterns from three to thirty feet high, depending on the size of pool and fountain. Light the pool or fountain at night to add to your enjoyment. Place a light below the water in the pool to make it glow. Light in fixtures that look like lily pads are available. For a jet, there are spotlights in white or color to play on frolicking water.

127

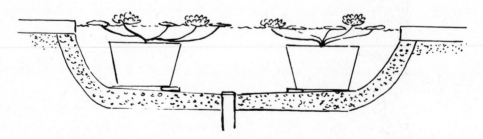

A reflecting pool with a small weeping tree makes a restful feature for a patio, and waterlilies grown in tubs in the pool make spots of color.

Paley Park in New York City (Zion & Breen, L.A.). *Osmundson photo*

Two views of a sheltered patio of oriental style. Designed by C. M. Harrington, Jr. *Photography by Wells*

In a California patio, jets of water spurt from basins on three levels, making delightful music. The featured plants are those of bold silhouette—philodendron, palm, aloe, papyrus. *Hort-Pix*

Many types of garden figures are available for patio fountains, and a pool does not have to be large to be effective. *Photography by Wells*

ORNAMENTS

Beauty of detail always gives a sense of taste and quality. The smaller the area, the more important it is to have accessories in proper scale. Ornaments, useful or decorative, should also be appropriate, not overwhelming. Place animal figures as if they were in their habitat. Set a contemporary statue where its bold form will stand out. Don't overdo, especially on a small patio. One lovely piece is far better than a number of miscellaneous objects.

Among the most charming accessories for the average patio are birdbaths and bird feeders. A large fluted shell or simple shallow bowl can serve as a birdbath. Place it under a tree or at the edge of a flower border. It need not always be on a pedestal. Hang feeders from trees or set them on posts.

There are ornaments for all sorts of patios, intricate Victorian plant stands to hold an array of potted plants, graceful wrought-iron tables, large ceramic urns to nestle in a bed of low evergreens, or a shining carboy, a large glass jar, to brighten a flower border. A sundial is an interesting ornament for a sunny patio.

Try your hand at making ceramic or stained-glass wall plaques or ceramic figures and free-form fountains. An unusual piece of driftwood or a beautiful rock, souvenirs of a trip, make delightful ornaments.

This free-form sculpture is a fountain with a drip falling on three levels. A circulating pump makes the most of a small amount of water. Designed by Gay McDonnell. *Photography by Wells*

An interesting planting, accented with a fine piece of sculpture, makes a delight-ful foreground for the view from this rooftop terrace. Glass in the railing miti-gates the force of wind without obstructing the view. Note the many variations in texture in the planting. *Molly Adams photo*

Contemporary statues for a patio need a plain background to set off their bold lines. *Photography by Wells*

FURNISHINGS AND GAMES

The furniture you select should be comfortable, weatherproof, and, of course, harmonious. Get plastic covers to put over cushioned pieces in bad weather. The latest addition to outdoor living is weatherproof carpeting; it comes in various colors, and is especially nice on concrete floors and around swimming pools.

Awnings also come in many colors and patterns and with different trimmings. They can be made up in any shape or size. They are practical, supplying shade and protection from rain when needed.

A deck can have the airy feeling of being among treetops, especially when a tree grows up through it. The railing with a bench makes a secure edge. *Molly Adams photo*

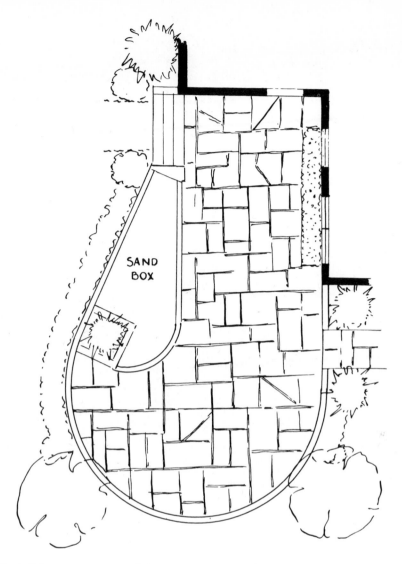

SAND
BOX

Small children enjoy a sand box on a patio. This one is planned to become a flower bed when its usefulness as a sand box is over.

For small children the paved patio or terrace is a good play place, particularly when the ground is damp. It is also close enough to the house to be kept in view. Plan space for a sand box (later it can be turned into a flower bed); or make a temporary square sand box that can be covered over in the evening for use as a low table.

Smooth cement paving is good for shuffle board, and fine for dancing. Squares for checkers or chess can be painted or set into the pavement. All these thoughtful details make the patio an inviting place.

Cascades of morning-glory and ivy adorn the railings of this balcony deck, and the slatted fence protects the plantings from wind. *George Taloumis photo*

Outdoor carpeting makes the concrete floor of a patio more comfortable, and space left between fence and carpet makes the area appear larger. The trees behind the fence assure privacy. Original wall plaques decorate the interesting fence design. Designed by Gay McDonnell.

Part Two

ROOF GARDENS

A circular planter on a brick rooftop terrace is built out from the wall to set off the planting and make a place for a small shade tree. *Hort-Pix*

11

Designing a Garden in the Sky

TO SEE SOMETHING GROWING gives a lift to life, and this is especially true in a big city. Fortunately you do not need land and lots of space and many plants to have an attractive garden. A small city roof garden properly planned can be a charming oasis in the midst of concrete and brick, and a garden in the sky is as important as on the ground. However, city gardeners are often so thrilled to see *anything* green growing on a roof top that they turn terraces into a veritable jungle of foliage.

A curved brick planter, more than two feet deep, holds enough soil for a permanent planting of crabapple-trees and a border of teucrium, with chrysanthemums, ferns, and other plants in between. The white finial, one of a pair, is a good accent in the midst of so much brick. *George Taloumis photo*

Roof gardening is an artificial form of gardening, and this should be taken into account in your planning. There are many tricks to getting plants to perform well on a rooftop. Employ these with ingenuity to make a garden that not only has an abundance of color and foliage but an interesting design as well.

Roof gardens are of four types. There are the tiny balconies, the larger terraces on the set-backs of modern buildings, gardens covering the entire roof of a city house or a garage, and spacious penthouse gardens at the top of the list, both literally and figuratively.

All these gardens have the same problems. They are limited in space, some much more than others. There is usually strong wind to cope with, deep shade or very hot sun, and reflected heat from many buildings. The choice of plants is restricted to those that will grow in large tubs or plant boxes, and can endure city fumes and smog. All this seems to act as a challenge to the many city gardeners who take pride in making really lovely gardens in the sky.

A deep permanent cement planter in the corner of a large rooftop is accented by a white statue and holds yew and a flowering crabapple-tree. The high wall offers excellent protection from wind. *George Taloumis photo*

Balcony Gardens

Balcony gardens are so small they must depend on plants in window boxes or in pots fastened to railings or walls. Since floor space is at a premium, keep your gardening up on the sides as far as possible. Plants in hanging baskets will add a profusion of color, and vines can festoon the balcony edge all summer. A pink or red geranium on a coffee table makes a gay accent.

Wind is ever a problem on balconies. Try to protect your planting boxes with low fencing that will let air through, but still break the force of the wind. A trellis gives good protection to a vine.

In this roof garden, there is a comfortable open sunny area and a shaded section protected by a slatted trellis covered with Fiberglas. *Roche photo*

TERRACES

Terraces on modern buildings are usually planned by architects so that there are adequate parapets and good drainage. Two problems are thus settled in advance. But the shape of the terrace is apt to be long and narrow, a difficult space to make into an attractive design and the smaller the space, the more important is the design. Get out paper and pencil, if you do not plan to have professional help, and sketch out some ideas. Your design should be definite and uncluttered, with a form that will be pleasing in winter after the flowers are gone.

Any visual trick that will make a narrow space seem wider is a help. Circular lines always fool the eye, diagonal lines also. Cutting off one end of a long narrow space with an arbor or awning shortens the length and also provides a much needed shady spot and privacy from above. A row of broad shrubs, such as forsythia or Russian-olive, at one end would also shorten the length. Breaking the space about two-thirds of the way along with a tree or feature is another trick.

When it cannot be found elsewhere, space for outdoor living and plants can be created, as on the roof of this carport. *George Taloumis photo*

140

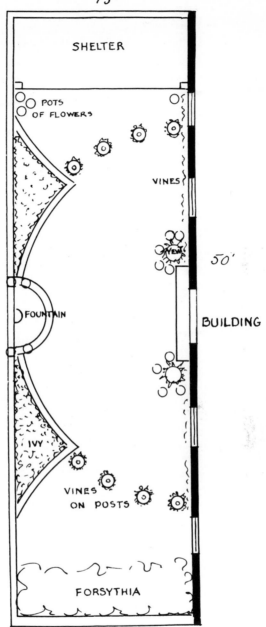

15'

SHELTER

POTS OF FLOWERS

VINES

YEW

50'

FOUNTAIN

BUILDING

IVY

VINES ON POSTS

FORSYTHIA

This design is for a fifteen-by fifty-foot patio and shows what a radial design can do to increase the feeling of space.

On most terraces, plants must grow in tubs or boxes. These can be built in any size to fit the design. For a ten-foot-wide terrace, boxes of a twelve-to-eighteen inch width are standard for the sides. Such boxes can be transported to another terrace if you should move.

Let your terrace garden express your individuality. Actually any kind from a formal rose garden to a vegetable garden is feasible.

141

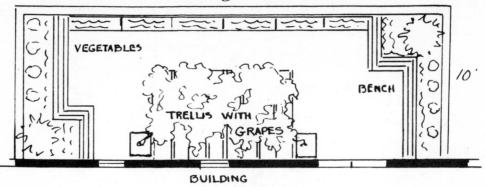

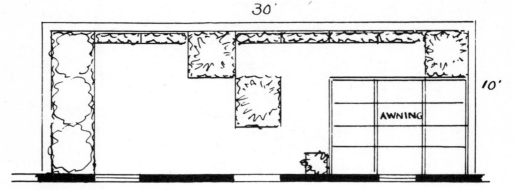

Benches add to the width of the beds at the ends of the upper design; a geometric feature interrupts the length of the lower design.

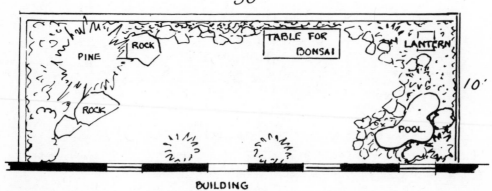

Breaking a design with diagonal lines fools the eye, making a narrow patio seem wider.

142

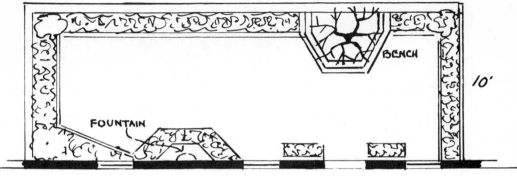

Another narrow patio, with bench and fountain features, is made to seem wider with diagonal lines.

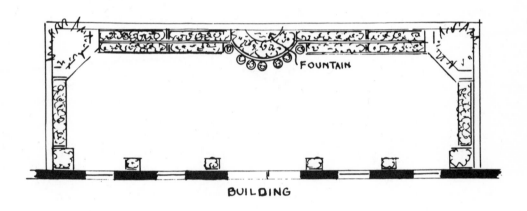

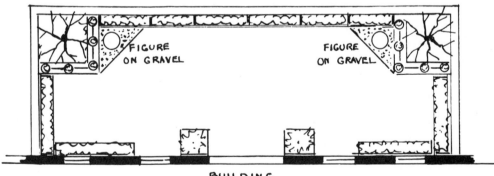

Two simple balanced plans for small terraces. The upper design has a fountain feature in the center of the long wall; the lower design includes figures at each end.

Roof Gardens

A typical roof garden has more space and so greater possibilities. However, care must be taken not to overload the roof of a house, and there must be good drainage not only for the whole roof, but for the containers also. Waterlogged soil is very heavy. Place large tubs with trees or shrubs where there are bearing walls underneath. This generally means at the corners or along the sides of a building. An architect or city engineer can advise you more exactly.

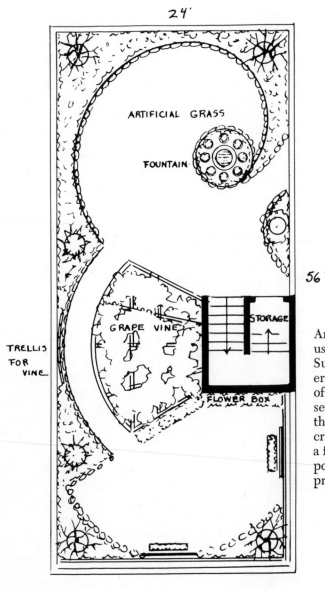

Artificial grass makes a useful roof-garden lawn. Surround it with Featherock, enclosing a mulch of wood chips in which to set pots of ivy. Decorate the corners with flowering crabapple trees and make a feature of a fountain with pots of flowers. The trellis provides shade.

144

Shade is especially welcome on a rooftop, which may be open to sun on all sides. Since most roof gardens cannot have a shade tree, a trellis or an awning is necessary for comfort. Make the trellis part of the structural design, and add a foliage pattern by covering it with a vine. Plan for water and electric connections. A telephone connection saves running up and down stairs, and a dumb-waiter can be a great help in getting up supplies. You might even have space for a cold frame or a very small greenhouse.

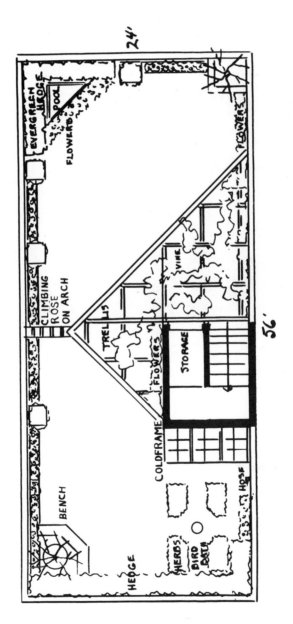

The stair covering serves as a base for a trellis that divides the roof garden in two with an arbor leading from one side to the other.

Penthouse Gardens

Penthouse gardens being larger and of varied shapes offer more possibilities for design. Rooftops are strong and well drained. Deep permanent planting beds with brick or concrete edges can be built. More shrubs and trees are possible. Select your plant materials for visual impact, thinking of them as units of design rather than as just something green.

These gardens are seen from windows throughout the year, so plan a winter as well as a summer picture. Penthouse gardens are extensions of the indoor living area. Make them livable and easy to care for as well as beautiful.

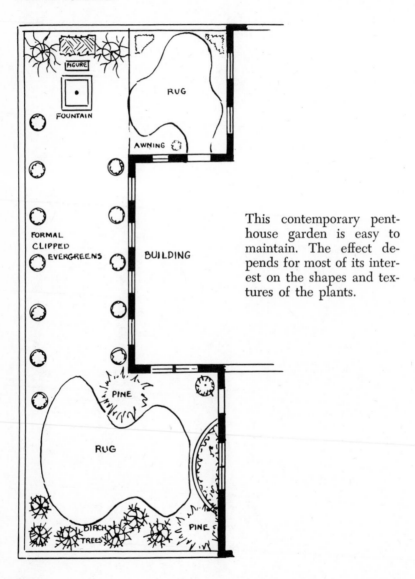

This contemporary penthouse garden is easy to maintain. The effect depends for most of its interest on the shapes and textures of the plants.

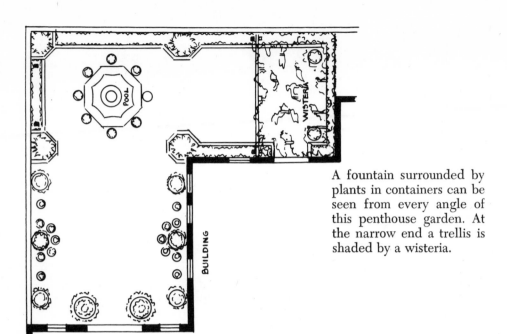

A fountain surrounded by plants in containers can be seen from every angle of this penthouse garden. At the narrow end a trellis is shaded by a wisteria.

A trellis covered with slats breaks the length of the terrace. At the far end is a picturesque small tree and vines on a fence. In the front corner, a free-form planter is on two levels. A weeping willow gives height and low spreading junipers grow on the lower level. A Japanese black pine with ivy offers another contrast of foliage. Color can be added by sinking pots of flowers among the evergreens and ivy.

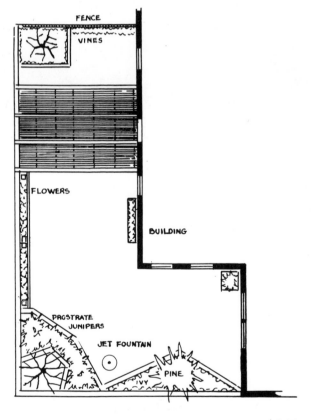

12

Constructing the Roof Garden

A ROOF GARDEN begins from the roof up instead of from the ground up. Every single thing including soil and plants must be carried there. In most cases, the only way plants can be grown is in containers, which may be built-in beds, boxes, pots, or jars.

Pots, tubs, and planters come in various sizes and shapes. In the long boxes here andromeda flourishes; and a redwood tub holds a flowering crabapple-tree. *George Taloumis photo*

On large terraces and penthouses, where roofs are supported by high parapets and good drainage has been provided, permanent beds for trees and shrubs can be constructed. Brick walls are the easiest to build. For curved walls, bricks can be laid on end to make a wall two inches wide, thus using up little space. Cement bricks weigh less than standard bricks, and four-inch-wide cement blocks make good straight walls. You can fill the hollows in them with plants or cap them with bricks. Allow "weep holes" every three to four feet. Of course, never place a bed over the roof drain itself.

Keep everything as light and strong as possible. For stone walls there is a lightweight durable porous stone called Featherock. This is ideal for roof-garden work. It comes in sizes from small stones to boulders, also as a veneer for cut-stone walls. The colors are silver-gray, charcoal, tan, and gray-brown. You can cut and shape it, drill holes in it for plants or water pipes.

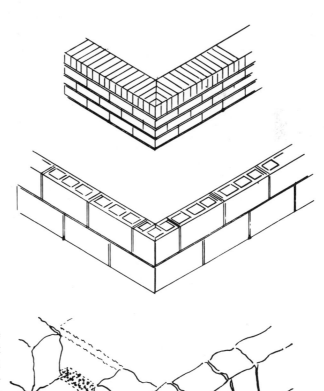

Permanent edgings can be made of brick four or eight inches wide, or of four-inch cement blocks and Featherock. Leave a weep hole every three or four feet. Spread stones over the bottom of a bed for drainage and a mulch on top to retain moisture.

Portable Planters

Portable planting boxes and tubs are suitable for any roof garden, but on smaller terraces and roofs which were not constructed to hold much weight, portable containers *must* be used. For narrow places, select a twelve-inch width. Planting boxes and tubs can be found readymade in a variety of shapes, sizes, and materials, or you can build them yourself.

Plants grow well in wooden containers that allow moisture and air to penetrate to roots, and wood is reasonably lightweight. There are long boxes for hedges or flower borders or round, square, hexagonal, or even triangular ones to fit the various angles of a design. Large wooden tubs make perfect planters for trees. Nail kegs make good and attractive planters, if you can find them. Always support planters above the floor to insure good drainage.

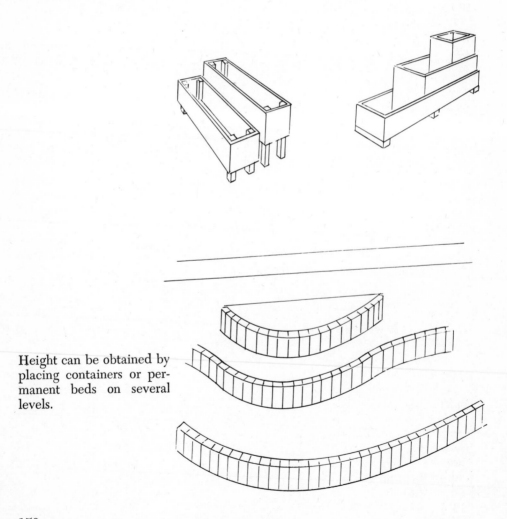

Height can be obtained by placing containers or permanent beds on several levels.

There are very lightweight Fiberglas planters that are almost unbreakable. Use them in shade, for they are inclined to heat up in the sun. Metal ones have the same disadvantage.

Ceramic and clay pots come in various decorative shapes and are attractive enough to keep in full view. To prevent excessive evaporation, put the smaller clay pots inside larger ones with a layer of mulch between, or place pots in a bed of mulch. The Italian-style concrete boxes are said to be heavy enough to stay in place on top of a wall, but never put anything on top of a wall that might conceivably fall off.

A stout structural framework with strips of canvas awning gives just enough shade for a rooftop terrace. The continuing design of sides and top creates an unusual design. *Canvas Awning Institute*

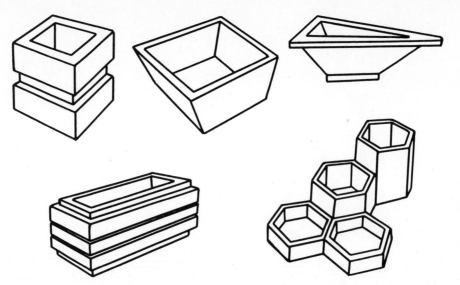

Wooden containers come in many shapes. For a group of them, it is a good idea to use a cluster of the same shape but of different heights.

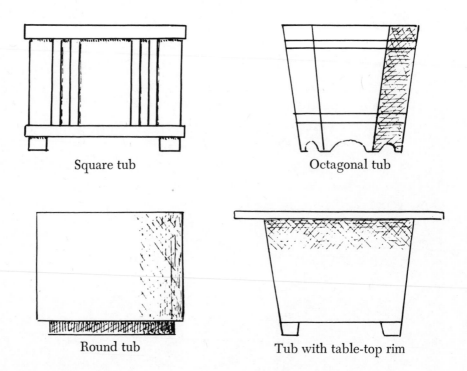

Square tub

Octagonal tub

Round tub

Tub with table-top rim

Large tubs for trees come in various shapes. One has a broad rim that can serve as a table.

Most hanging baskets are of wire with a moss lining, but there is a new green plastic one on the market with double walls that hold water in between. With these you need water plants only every ten days. And no water spills out. Arrange any hanging basket so that you can lower it for easy watering; otherwise you must use a step-stool.

Soil and Water

Soil for roof-garden planters must be moisture retentive, but drain quickly. Soggy soil is not only heavy but unhealthy for plants. Over the bottom of every container, spread a layer of cinders, small stones or shards (broken pot pieces), one inch for a box twelve inches deep, and more for deeper planters. Next spread a layer of peat or sphagnum moss to keep the soil from sifting through. For planting, make a mixture of top soil, sand, peatmoss, perlite, and fertilizer. Soil conditioners like perlite lighten the weight of the total volume.

On the surface of the planter, put a layer of mulch to help keep the soil moist. Incidentally any city gardener will benefit from reading *The City Gardener* by Philip Truex. It is full of useful information on growing plants on rooftops and in city backyards.

Here again weight, or lack of it, is important. Shallow pools made of Fiberglas or a plastic skin stretched over a wooden frame and surrounded with Featherock are lightweight. A figure with a basin at its feet and a circulating pump to run the water is always attractive. You can also get circular metal containers with a jet fountain run electrically, and a wall fountain takes up little room and weighs little. Plan for hose connections on your roof garden. Daily watering is essential due to the high rate of evaporation in container gardening, and syringing plants with a hose helps keep them clean.

Screens and Flooring

The wind whistles around the corners of high buildings. Gardens situated there need protective screens. Shrubs like privet and trees with small leaves don't get whipped to pieces, and these can help to shield other plants. Fences that let air through, or panels of shatterproof glass with spaces between, or wrought-iron fences help to break the force of the wind. On some rooftops there are unsightly chimney pipes, water towers, or air vents. Trellises are useful in screening these from view. Where privacy is

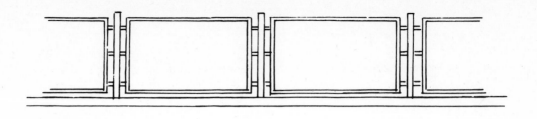

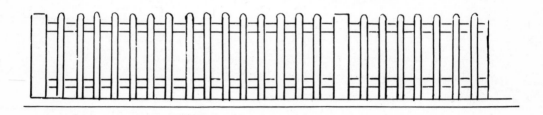

Screens are necessary for windbreaks but should not cut off all circulation of air. If the screen just breaks the force of the wind, it is helpful.

needed between one terrace and another, erect a stockade fence or one of split bamboo.

Where no permanent floor exists for a roof garden, there are various ways of making one. First of all be sure the roof itself is watertight and has good drainage. One possibility is to make a deck of duck boards. There is also a new liquid flooring that can be put on over wood or other surfaces to make a permanent, good-looking pavement of any size or shape. This is being used on public buildings.

154

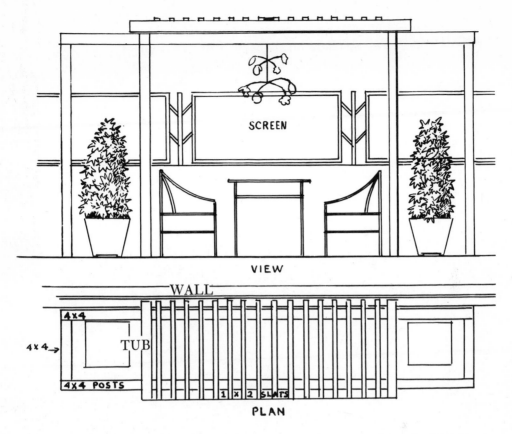

SCREEN

VIEW

WALL

4X4

4X 4 →

TUB

4X4 POSTS

1 x 2 SLATS

PLAN

A shaded place is pleasant on a sunny roof garden; it need not be large.

Pebbles make a floor of interesting texture if the area is not too large. And now we even have artificial grass, the kind that is being used to replace grass in ball parks and stadiums. There is also outdoor carpeting to cover an unsightly floor, and it is most attractive.

Shade and Care

Contrived shade is desirable on those sunny roofs where there can be no such thing as a large tree. Whatever shelter you build, make it durable and well secured. Awnings are excellent because on occasion they can be rolled up to let sun and rain get to the plants. They can also be colorful and decorative with scallops and fringe. A roof of wood strips and Fiberglas panels will also let some light through, and vines on a strong trellis give shade. Even a small arbor is pleasant when there is little space.

155

Roof gardens may need no lawn mowing, but they do have their own chores. Check on daily watering. Whether the plants need water or not, the floor, in fair weather, has to be hosed almost daily, at least in large cities where the deposit of dust, grit, and oil ash is continuous. For the

English ivy grows well on a fence that protects it from sun and wind. On a tiled rooftop terrace, bamboo and Japanese andromeda are a nice complement for the Oriental figure. *Molly Adams photo*

same reason the leaves of all plants will need regular rinsing. Fertilize every two weeks. Pick off dead flowers so that the garden always looks nice, and then plants will bloom better too. Every year, replace soil or at least top-dress it as deeply as possible without damaging roots. Prune when necessary to keep shrubs and trees shapely and in bounds.

The wavy lines of a corkscrew willow, *Salix matsudana,* make a very interesting and emphatic pattern. *George Taloumis photo*

Here a section of stockade fencing and tall shrubs makes a screen for a small rooftop terrace. Ivy in the planters stretches out to cover the whole parapet with green. *Molly Adams photo*

13

Planting the Roof Garden

PLANTS ON A ROOF GARDEN bear no relation to what is around them. They are surrounded either by limitless empty space that leads the eye too far away or by masses of concrete and glass with strong architectural vertical and horizontal lines. Plantings that look well on the ground do not have the same effect as those on a roof, so forget preconceived ideas, experiment with new ways of growing familiar plants. It is important to emphasize foregrounds with bright color or dramatic pattern to give a feeling of intimate enclosure, and also to make a screen, even an illusionary one, between your island of planting and the world beyond. A screen planting also breaks the force of the wind that continually batters roof gardens.

Space is at a premium. This means that any shrub or tree with a large spread is out, unless it is purposely needed to reduce a space that is too long and narrow, or like the useful privet, can be severely pruned. Fortunately, growing shrubs and trees in containers has a limiting effect on the size just as in bonsai culture. Since there is no room for masses of shrubbery, concentrate on quality and select a few fine specimens.

Think of plants for their form, for their texture of branch and foliage, as well as their durability on a rooftop. A tree, such as a dogwood or thornless locust, with horizontally branching patterns, will offset nearby vertical lines of buildings. The soft flowing lines of a weeping willow will do the same. A tree with a picturesque irregular habit of growth, such as goldenrain, staghorn sumac, or 'Red Jade' crabapple will attract attention to itself.

VIEW

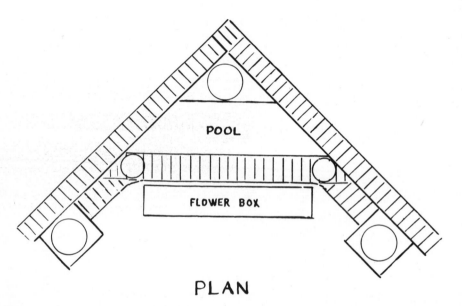

PLAN

On a tall building the foreground for the view should be bright and attractive. Here interest is found on several levels.

Multiple-stemmed trees or those that fork low can help to break up harsh lines. Gray birch and saucer magnolia are good examples. Where there are bands of strong horizontal lines in the background of your roof garden, use columnar or fastigiate varieties. There is a fastigiate gingko, a white pine, and a flowering cherry. The pyramidal hornbeam is another fine tree, and so is the new 'Doric' maple. All these trees will withstand city conditions and grow so narrowly as to take up very little room.

160

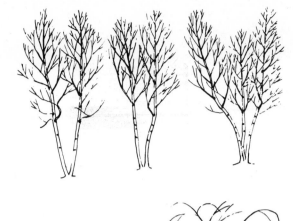

The winter structure of some trees contributes to the design of a roof garden. The branches soften the strong architectural lines of nearby buildings.

Because privet does so well on rooftops, it is used with monotous regularity. True, it does stand shearing into a dense form, or it can be left to grow into a loose mass up to fifteen feet. A more interesting hedge shrub is the winged euonymus. The brilliant raspberry-red fall hue and intriguing corky-cinnamon–colored bark in winter bring a welcome warmth of color. Forsythia with its early yellow blossoms also does well on a roof, and flowering-quince is excellent as a hedge plant or specimen. Imagine a hedge of silvery Russian-olive with crimson roses or petunias in front of it! The beautiful evergreen abelia with pink summer flowers is in every way a desirable shrub.

It seems that plants which do well along the sea coast will also tolerate city conditions on a roof. This is true of white pine, and the picturesque Japanese black pine. Red-cedar and its varieties stand wind and sun, but are very susceptible to injury from red-spider. The beautiful dark green yews need some protection. Plant them in sheltered corners where there is some shade. Yucca, a desert plant, makes a dramatic specimen in a tub with its spiky evergreen leaves and great candelabrum of white flowers in July.

161

TREES FOR THE ROOF GARDEN

Flowering crabapples	*Malus* in variety
Flowering dogwood	*Cornus florida*
Gingko	*Gingko biloba*
Goldenchain-tree	*Laburnum vossi*
Goldenrain-tree	*Koelreuteria paniculata*
Gray birch	*Betula populifolia*
Japanese maple	*Acer palmatum*
Moraine locust	*Robinia pseudo-acacia* 'Moraine'
Mountain-ash	*Sorbus aucuparia*
Pyramidal hornbeam	*Carpinus betulus pyramidalis*
Red maple	*Acer rubrum*
Russian-olive	*Elaeagnus angustifolia*
Silk-tree	*Albizzia julibissin*
Weeping willow	*Salix babylonica*

SHRUBS THAT THRIVE

Abelia	*Abelia grandiflora*
Andromeda	*Pieris japonica*
Bush honeysuckle	*Lonicera tatarica*
Cotoneaster	*Cotoneaster* in variety
Enkianthus	*Enkianthus perulatus*
Euonymus	*Euonymus* in variety
Firethorn	*Pyracantha lalandi*
Floribunda roses	*Rosa* hybrids
Flowering-quince	*Chaenomeles lagenaria*
Forsythia	*Forsythia* in variety
Japanese holly	*Ilex rotund*
Mock-orange	*Philadelphus* in variety
Privet	*Ligustrum* in variety
Pussy willow	*Salix discolor*
Rose-of-Sharon	*Hibiscus syriacus*
Sumac	*Rhus hirta*
Tamarisk	*Tamarix pentandra*

TOLERANT EVERGREENS

Mugho pine	*Pinus mugo mughus*
Norway spruce	*Picea excelsa*
Scotch pine	*Pinus sylvestris*
White pine	*P. strobus*
Yew	*Taxus* in variety

162

VALUE OF VINES

Think of what you can do with a vine on a rooftop! You can cover a blank wall, make a screen on a trellis, shade an arbor, soften the edge of a planter, or make decorative patterns on a wall to frame accessories. You can train vines on posts as pylons, or make them into swags of color. A sweet potato, its tip in a glass of water, will produce a luxuriant vine. With so little room the more vertical designing you can do the more beautiful your roof garden will be.

On a rooftop terrace, plants grown in separate containers flourish: rubber-tree, bougainvillea (trained to form an arch), cannas, and needle asparagus. Most of them can be moved around to suggest a path, as here, or to make other demarcations. The various growth patterns are well set off by the white wall. *George Taloumis photo*

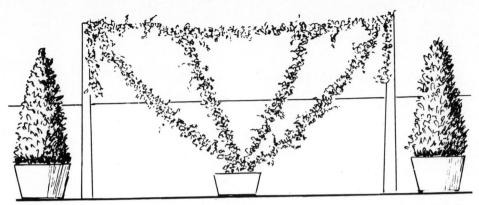

A vine can be trained into a swag to make an effective silhouette against the sky.

English ivy burns if exposed to sun. Plant it on a shady protected wall or use it as a ground-cover in shade. Euonymus is a better evergreen vine for sunny areas. Boston-ivy is a neat grower. After the gorgeously colored leaves fall, a delicate tracery of stems remain to decorate the wall.

Vines—wisteria, grape, and silver-lace—relieve the hard lines of necessary fences and parapets.

Baltic ivy	*Hedera helix baltica*
Bittersweet	*Celastrus scandens*
Boston-ivy	*Parthenocissus tricuspidata*
Chinese wisteria	*Wisteria sinensis*
Climbing rose 'Blaze'	*Rosa 'Blaze'*
Grape	*Vitis*
Honeysuckle	*Lonicera* in variety
Perennial sweet-pea	*Lathyrus latifolius*
Silver-lace-vine	*Polygonum auberti*
Virginia-creeper	*Parthenocissus quinquefolia*

Flowers

Bulbs and annuals along with such potted perennials as chrysanthemums supply the bright colors so necessary to a roof garden. All do well in planting boxes and pots. Geraniums are about the most popular and carefree of flowering plants. Petunias and marigolds thrive and bloom all summer. For trailing beauty, plant verbena and lantana. You can set out annuals a week or two earlier on the roof than in the ground, and also plant them closer together.

Potted houseplants—ferns, rosary-vine, geraniums, and others—hung on a fence on one side of a roof garden make an attractive display and give the plants a healthy summer vacation. A wisteria and a flowering-maple grow well in jardinieres. The table holds an angel-wing begonia and a collection of succulents. *George Taloumis photo*

Where space is at a premium, vines planted between fence posts give a lot of green in a small area. Perennial sweetpea and everblooming honeysuckle are good choices.

Planting boxes filled with annuals and trailing vines, with other vines trained above, give height of foliage and interest to a narrow space.

166

Grow flowers at levels where you can keep them well groomed, picking off dead blossoms daily. Fill boxes and tubs with trailing plants. Moneywort (*Lysimachia nummularia*) is ideal for planters. Baltic ivy is also good. For a bold accent grow a castor-bean in a tub. Plant flowers in boxes on several levels or on steps to make the most of available space, and splash every likely spot with color or green foliage. For a party, one can order pots of flowers in full bloom from the florist. Group them at focal points or plunge the pots into the mulch between low evergreens or ground-covers.

Raised beds, flower boxes—set in a design of different heights on a wall—and espaliered trees are good planting devices where space is limited as in a city terrace, on the ground or in the sky. Here white tulips are followed by yellow lantanas. The pale pink geraniums and ivy are attractive all summer, also the evergreen andromeda at the left. *George Taloumis photo*

Even Vegetables and Herbs

Vegetables and herbs are fun to grow on a roof too. Tomatoes or pole beans tied to strong posts make high accents. Underplant them with lettuce followed by parsley and carrots. There is a climbing spinach that will poke its way up through a wire or wood trellis. It comes from India and likes hot weather. What could be more decorative than flowering kale, or more delicious if you can bear to pick it.

Gray-green herbs stand drought and heat well. Lavender with its pleasant fragrance and teucrium both make charming low borders. Thyme is a gray woolly herb to soften the edge of a planter, and the aromatic artemisias, which spread so fast on the ground, do very well when contained in a box. A plant of rosemary is handsome, but it is tender and must be taken indoors in winter. Chives are always welcome, and some dill will add color. Don't forget the decorative strawberry either in a strawberry jar or as an edging plant. You can combine flowers and vegetables for an attractive and colorful effect.

Even tomatoes like these and dwarf fruit trees can be grown by a rooftop farmer. *Pan American Seed Co.*

14

Decorations for the Roof Garden

SINCE THE PURPOSE OF A ROOF GARDEN is to have as much verdure and flower as possible in limited and artificial conditions, it is logical to include some striking and unusual plants. These will be the best decorations rather than sculpture and man-made objects.

A hanging basket of lavender ivy geraniums on the edge of an awning and a large planter accommodating yew, andromeda, and English ivy are kept healthy with frequent hosing and feeding. *George Taloumis photo*

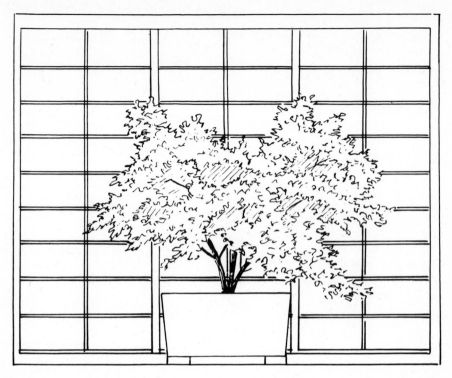

A beautiful specimen plant, as a Japanese maple, is silhouetted against a Japanese screen made of translucent plastic or Fiberglas.

PLANTS AS FEATURES

There are several ways of featuring plants. You can choose plants that are dramatically beautiful in line or foliage all year long. The Japanese maple (*Acer palmatum*) with lacy red leaves and irregular lines is distinctive. 'Red Jade' crabapple is a small tree with picturesque and rather pendent branches covered with blush-white flowers in spring and tiny bright red apples in fall. The larger varieties of cotoneaster and flowering-quince, with a little trimming, make unusual specimen plants. For a terrace seen only in summer the annual castor-bean is useful, growing quickly into a large plant with bold emphatic leaves. (The seeds are poisonous if eaten.) Caladiums are very decorative, in a shaded place protected from high winds.

Many shrubs are available trained into a standard or single-trunk form, and are highly decorative. There are tree roses, tree wisterias, and standard forms of golden privet, *Euonymus radicans vegetus,* and *Viburnum juddi.*

170

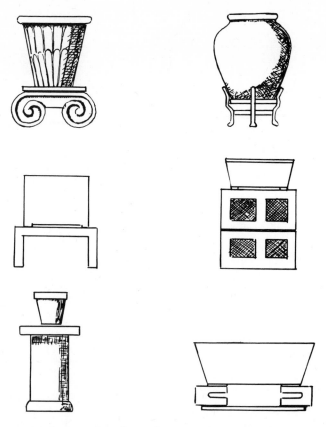

Containers are raised on pedestals to feature plants. Cement blocks and sewer tiles make good platforms.

You can give importance to plants by elevating containers on pedestals or by silhouetting them against a screen, fence, or blank wall. And there are attractive holders for suspending pots from walls, and hanging baskets for a cascade of flowers.

PLANTS FOR EMPHASIS

Another way to use plants saliently is to let them focus attention on an architectural or sculptured ornament. Group pots of bright geraniums or chrysanthemums around the base of a fountain. Let a planting of clipped dark green yew or boxleaf holly (*Ilex crenata convexa*) set off the solid forms of a statue. The flowing lines of a weeping tree make a contrasting background for a carving of clear and firm outline. Train vines to frame a wall plaque, or let them ramble over a large expanse of wall in their own natural patterns.

171

A setting for a figure is framed and accentuated by foreground planting.

An elaborate wrought-iron holder for flower pots decorates a large wall.

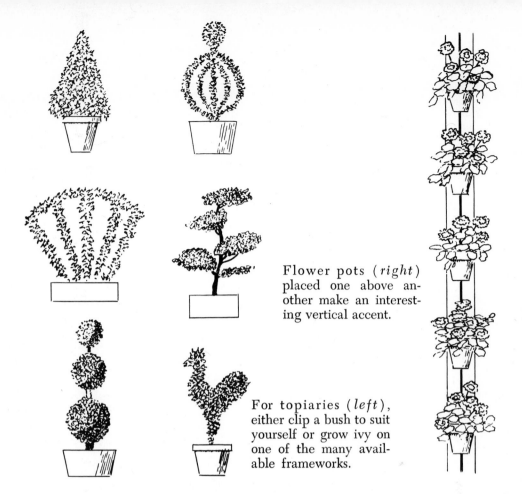

Flower pots (*right*) placed one above another make an interesting vertical accent.

For topiaries (*left*), either clip a bush to suit yourself or grow ivy on one of the many available frameworks.

TOPIARIES AND ESPALIERS

A third way of making plants decorative is to prune them into shapes as modern as tomorrow or as quaint as yesterday. With no lawn to mow or weeds to pull, you can take time to experiment with topiary work, the art of trimming trees or shrubs into various forms. Privet, boxwood, and Japanese holly all stand hard shearing into dense shapes. Baltic ivy can be trained on wire frames or grown in moss-filled forms to make interesting figures. You can also train some small trees, particularly fruit trees, and some shrubs flat against a wall in formal patterns.

Colorful containers make vivid contrasts with flower colors, as well as with evergreens. Paint tubs and boxes to match awnings or a screen. Set pots of flowers on a colorful outdoor rug. Use three shades of one color of one flower, or graduated sizes of plants. One of the advantages of a roof garden is that the smaller tubs can be readily moved to make new arrangements, and any planting which has passed its peak of bloom can be quickly replaced with something to bloom later on or already in bloom.

173

INDEX

INDEX